C Programming For Complete Beginners

Nourx N. Wilson

All rights reserved. Copyright © 2023 Nourx N. Wilson

COPYRIGHT © 2023 Nourx N. Wilson

All rights reserved.

No part of this book must be reproduced, stored in a retrieval system, or shared by any means, electronic, mechanical, photocopying, recording, or otherwise, without written permission from the publisher.

Every precaution has been taken in the preparation of this book; still the publisher and author assume no responsibility for errors or omissions. Nor do they assume any liability for damages resulting from the use of the information contained herein.

Legal Notice:

This book is copyright protected and is only meant for your individual use. You are not allowed to amend, distribute, sell, use, quote or paraphrase any of its part without the written consent of the author or publisher.

Introduction

Dive into the world of game programming with this guide. This guide provides you with a step-by-step journey through the process of creating a game, specifically focusing on the classic game 'Asteroids.' Whether you're a beginner or have some programming experience, this guide will help you understand the basics of C programming while applying your knowledge to the exciting realm of game development.

Get acquainted with the essentials of C programming, including an introduction to computers, operating systems, and how they run programs. Explore concepts like files, bytes, math, and variables, as well as the numeric types and operators essential for game programming. Learn about pointers, arrays, functions, and the struct data type, which form the building blocks of your game's functionality.

Discover the architecture of C programs, headers and library files, and external libraries such as the SDL2 library, which enables graphics and resource management in your game. Follow along with step-by-step instructions for installing SDL2 and setting up your project environment.

Delve into the intricacies of game loops, high precision timing, graphics, and text manipulation. Learn how to incorporate images, handle keyboard input, and implement game elements like spaceships, bullets, and asteroids. Understand collision detection, masks, and the principles of object-oriented programming through your game's development.

Master various techniques for debugging, optimizing, and improving your game, ensuring smooth gameplay and a rewarding player experience. From basic concepts to advanced game programming, this book equips you with the knowledge and skills to create your very own game and embark on a thrilling journey into the world of programming and game development.

Contents

Chapter 1. Introduction to C programming 1
The Game – Asteroids...2
Chapter 2. Computers and Operating Systems 3
Computers run programs all the time 3
Switching on a Computer 4
Operating Systems 5
Disk Drives 5
Windows 7/8/10 etc. 6
Computer Programs 6
Chapter 3. Running Programs 7
Files and Extensions 8
File Explorer 8
Chapter 4. Bytes and Bobs and some Maths 10
A Little bit of Math(s) 11
Octal 14
Files are bytes too! 15
More about Bytes 15
What's a signed number in hexadecimal? 16
Multiple Byte numbers 16
Chapter 5. Hello World 18
Listing of Hello World 18
Command Line Window? 20
Downloading Files 22
Projects 25

Game Source Code	25
Chapter 7. Our first project	26
Printing on Multiple Lines	33
Chapter 8. Variables in C	34
What is a Variable?	35
Numeric types for variables	36
How big are variables of a specified type?	36
Snippets	39
Unsigned types	40
Floating Point variables	41
Chapter 9. Another type: char	44
C Strings	44
What is a Pointer variable?	45
Chapter 10. A little Bit of C code	48
More Code	49
Programming Mistakes in C	50
TIP	51
Chapter 11. A Quick Overview of Visual Studio	52
Jumping backwards and forwards	54
Adding or Removing files from a Solution	55
Chapter 12. Array variables	58
Working with arrays	58
Accessing and using arrays	59
Counting from 0	61
Multiple dimension arrays	61
Text case in C	62
Comments	62

Chapter 13. Loop the loops 65
For Loop 65
The loop variable 67
A shortcut way of incrementing 69
Before or after ++? 69
Back to the for-loop 71
Empty and infinite loops 72
What it does 74
Chapter 14. More loops 75
The Bool type 76
The Do Loop 78
The Goto statement 78
Nested loops 80
Chapter 15. About operators. 82
Numeric Operators 82
Comparison operators 82
The ternary operator ?: 83
Logical and Binary Ands 83
Logical And / Or 83
Binary-and, Binary-Or and Exclusive-Or 85
Chapter 16 - Structs 87
Type names 87
Explaining struct declarations 88
Structs and arrays 90
typedefs 92
Chapter 17. Functions. 94
Function Layout 95

What is a void function? 96

Function Declarations 96

A few notes on functions. 98

Chapter 18. More about functions. 100

Stack memory 100

Heap Memory 101

Why not 64-bit? 102

Function parameters 102

The return type 103

The return statement. 103

Return in void/non-void functions 104

You don't need a return in a void function. 105

Chapter 19. Pointers 106

Arrays and Pointers 111

Viewing memory during debug in Visual Studio 116

No _ADDRESSOF? 117

Hiding the Memory view Window 118

Chapter 20. Text Strings 119

Safe and Unsafe C string functions 122

What is a buffer? 123

Chapter 21. The Asteroids Game 125

Spaceship controls 125

Special keys 125

The Source Code 126

Chapter 22. Architecture of C Programs 128

Header and Lib files 128

External Libraries 129

Chapter 23. Graphics 130
SDL2 Library 130
Game Resources 131
Chapter 24. Installing SDL2 134
Downloading Files from the Internet 134
32- Bit or 64-Bit? 136
Checklist 136
dll folder files 137
lib folder files 137
Include folder files 138
Setting up an empty C project 138
Configuring your project 139
Adding Libraries to a C or C++ project 140
Chapter 25. An SDL Demo program 144
Files for this chapter 148
Chapter 26. The Game Loop 149
Flipping the screen 152
What does that mean? Double buffered? 152
Flipping What? 152
Faster, much faster! 152
Chapter 27. High Precision Timing 154
The hr_time library 154
How does timing work? 156
Chapter 28. Drawing Text. 158
Images 159
A Bit About Compiling Visual Studio Solutions 162
What is an Escape Char? 163

Printing numbers on screen	164
The function printch	166
Visual Studio lets you view and edit image files	166
How It Works	169
How long is a frame in time?	170
Files for this chapter	174
Chapter 29. More Game Elements	175
The player's ship.	175
The Switch statement	177
Key Handling	181
GameLoop and ProcessEvents	182
Ship Movements	182
Rotating the Ship	183
Velocity in two dimensions	185
The ApplyThrust function	186
The MoveplayerShip function	186
Files for this chapter	190
Chapter 30. Adding in asteroids	191
Asteroid Graphics	192
Files for this chapter	195
Chapter 31. Adding in bullets	196
Why countdown and ttl?	198
Files for this chapter	198
Chapter 32. A bit of C99.	199
Comments in C	200
Chapter 33. Editing with Visual Studio.	201
Navigate by function.	201

Bookmarks	201
Refactoring.	203
Chapter 34. Restructuring	205
About Header files	206
Examples of pre-processor directives	207
Include Guards	207
The lib.h file	209
Files for this chapter	211
Chapter 35 Show the Score	212
Showing Lives	212
What is a Version Control System (VCS)?	213
Adding lives etc.	214
InitSetup Change	215
Pause Key and Hyperspace Jump	216
Files for this chapter	219
Chapter 36. Explosions	220
Determining Asteroid Velocities	226
Show me the explosions!	226
Files for this chapter	227
Chapter 37. Sounds	228
SDL_Mixer	228
Using SDL_mixer	229
The sound code	229
Files for this chapter	233
Chapter 38. Detecting Collisions Part 1	234
How do the masks work?	236
Generating the Masks	236

Testing the Mask generation 238
The mask output 240
Text Files 241
C multi-dimensional arrays and row ordering 241
Resource Manager 245
Files for this chapter 245
Chapter 39. Detecting Collisions Part 2 246
Checking for Collisions 247
Intersecting rectangles with SDL 248
Reducing Collision Checks 249
Objects and cells 251
Why do we add an object to cells? 251
Adding an object to a cell? 252
Processing Cells 252
Checking Each Cell 253
Objects in a Cell 254
Adding a pointer into a list of pointers in a cell 255
How many cells does an object cover? 257
Pointers and arrows 259
Back to the Cells 260
Timing ClearCellList 260
Chapter 40. Detecting Collisions Part 3 263
Chapter 41. Passing Parameters into functions 266
Using ++ with pointers 268
Why are pointers so important? 268
When to use & and when not to 270
Chapter 42. Detecting Collisions Part 4 274

The Overlap function	276
Destroying Objects	283
How much processing time does it take?	284
Viewing the overlap pixels	284
Files for this chapter	286
Chapter 43. Ever Wondered about if (!value)	287
Chapter 44. Some Debugging Tips	291
More Logging	291
Show me the cells	292
Files for this chapter	295
Chapter 45. Improving the game	296
Scores	296
A really stupid bug	304
A bug fixing Strategy	306
Files for this chapter	306
Chapter 46. Adding Level Structure	307
Making Life Easier for yourself	309
Adding Lives	312
Aliens?	315
Changes to Text Sprites	315
Game play problem	318
Yet another Bug!	319
Files for this chapter	320
Chapter 47. Alien Ships!	321
Alien Artificial intelligence	322
When is a function not a function?	323
Flashing Alien	324

Adding a Shield control	327
Drawing the Shield	328
Chapter 48. The High Score	331
Entering the High Score	337
Files for this chapter	341
Chapter 49. Finishing off	342
Running asteroids outside of Visual Studio	344

Chapter 1. Introduction to C programming

C is one of the older programming languages – by the year 2022 it will be fifty years old. There have been hundreds of programming languages invented since 1972, but C is still one of the most popular.

Much programming on Linux is still done in C and Linux itself is written in C. In this book though we'll be programming in C on Windows.

To understand what a programming language does, you need to know a little about a computer and computer programs. So before I look at C, read the next chapter on Computers and Operating Systems. If you know what a computer is then feel free to jump to chapter three.

If you only know how to run Windows programs by clicking on icons that's OK. I'll introduce you to command lines and show you how to type in commands.

Once we've built the game, you'll run it by clicking on icons. It's still Windows after all!

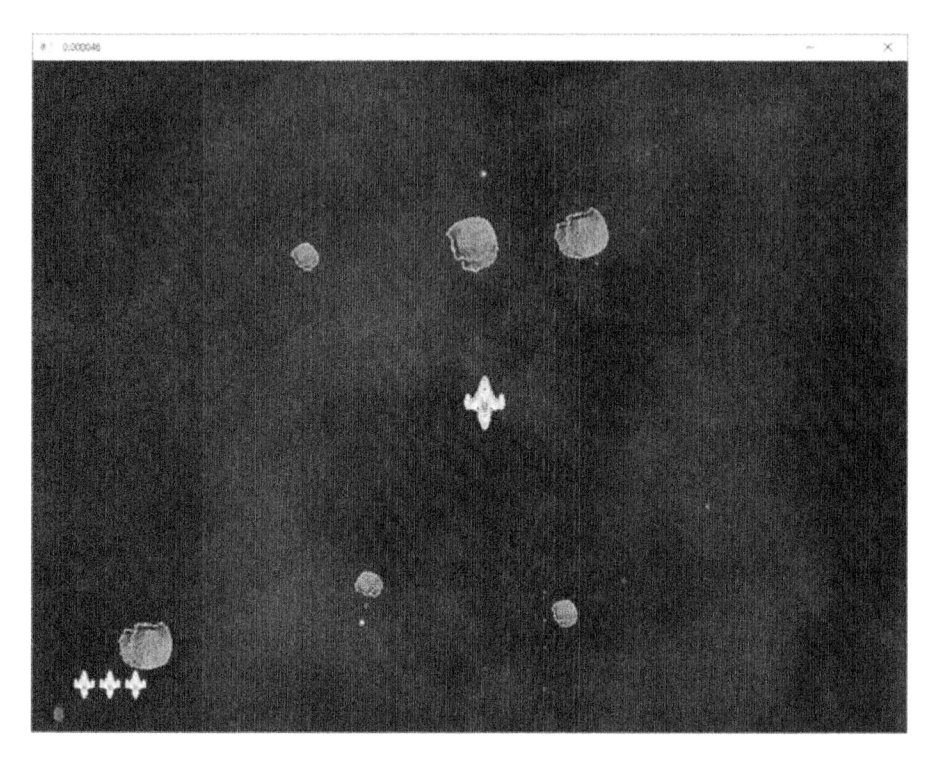

The Game – Asteroids

In this book, not only will I teach you how to program in C but I'll also show you how to create a full arcade like game loosely based on Atari's Asteroids™.

That's an image from the game above. It's my interpretation and looks quite different from the original game. Graphics are solid not wire-frame like in the original.

It runs at 60 frames per second even with hundreds of objects on screen at the same time.

Chapter 2. Computers and Operating Systems

A computer has a powerfulengine that can execute instructions at a rate of between 250 million and a billion instructions per second.

> RAM – Random Access memory

Computers also come with RAM (short for Random Access Memory) which is working memory and holds all instructions and data but loses them when you power off. When a program is run, it has to be loaded into RAM first then it is run.

Then there's ROM (short for Read-Only Memory) where the instructions are permanently stored. ROM instructions run when the computer is first turned on.

> ROM – Read-Only Memory

Computers run programs all the time

Everything you do on a computer is handled by a program. As the mouse cursor moves across the screen, a non-stop stream of mouse coordinates is received by a program. It's how Windows (or Linux or Mac OS) works.

When you double click an icon, the OS loads and runs/executes a program in RAM.

Switching on a Computer

Once the computer has started up - booted up in techy terms, it runs a program stored in ROM and that loads more programs and data from disk into RAM and starts running them. Disk can mean a hard disk, an SSD (Solid State Drive), a memory stick or even an SD Card. Raspberry Pi computers run on SD cards.

The process of booting up is what happens when your computer is turned on. During boot up various programs in ROM are run to check RAM, and make sure all the attached devices including keyboard and mouse are working OK.

Any external drives such as hard disks or memory sticks, devices such as headphones, mice, speakers are all initialised and then the rest of the operating system (more programs!) is loaded from disk into RAM.

Eventually it reaches the point where you enter your login details. If they are correct it loads your personalised settings. This includes things like themes and colours for the screen and all the short-cut icons for programs.

Everything that happens is because one or more computer programs have been run or are still running.

Operating Systems

All software that runs your computer after boot-up is called an operating system (OS). The main three OS are Windows, Mac and Linux. All do pretty much the same thing but look and behave quite differently. We'll look at running Windows programs in Chapter (Three) 'Running Programs'.

The OS reads the keyboard, moves the mouse cursor and handles things when you click or double click on an icon. Behind the scenes it also manages networking, files and folders and it frees up RAM when you close programs. It keeps everything running smoothly.

Disk Drives

Windows manages all your disk drives with the first one usually being the C: drive. It can sometimes be D: E: F: etc. but C: is the most common and usually the drive holding Windows programs. When you plug in a memory stick it gets the next available letter.

A: and B: are rarely used these days but before hard disks and SSDs were common, they were the names of floppy disk drives. Those have been replaced by USB memory drives, external SSDs and hard disks and are always given drive letters that start from C:.

Windows 7/8/10 etc.

In this book, I'll be running programs on Windows 10 but you might be running Windows 7 or maybe even an earlier version like XP. Windows 7 and Windows 10 between them account for about 90% of all current Windows installations worldwide.

Don't worry if you're not on Windows 10. The code I'll be showing you will run on Windows 7 or possibly even earlier. But the version of SDL2 we'll use may not work on Windows before 7.

Computer Programs

A computer program is a collection of instructions plus data and one or two other things and is stored in a file with an .exe extension. If you have Microsoft Excel or Word installed then those are just computer programs.

On your desktop, you'll see a collection of icons. If the icon has a little arrow in a white square in the bottom left corner like this then it's a short-cut to where the program is actually located. Most icons on a Windows desktop are short-cuts.

So programming is about creating computer programs and that's what you'll learn. In the next chapter we'll look at running programs.

Chapter 3. Running Programs

As I said in the last chapter a computer program on Windows is a file on disk with the file extension .exe. A file extension is the last part of a filename like .txt or .exe. By default on Windows, you don't see file extensions but it's very easy to configure it so you can see them.

Right click on the Start button (Move the mouse cursor over it and click the right mouse button) and then click (i.e. left click) File Explorer in the popup menu. You should see something like this below. I've highlighted File Explorer.

That runs the Windows File Explorer program and lets you see files and folders on your hard disk and other devices. A folder is just a place to keep files.

The top menu of File Explorer (shown on the next page) should say **File Home Share View** and you should click View. Windows 7 might be slightly different but just look for View on the top menu.

On Windows 10 a menu will appear, click Options on the right. This will open a small popup window called Folder Options with three Tabs: **General, View and Search**.

Now in the Folder Options window click on the View tab and in the advanced settings you'll see a load of options.

Look for Hidden Files and folders, about 6 lines down and make sure you click on Show hidden, files, folders and drives. Just a bit below where it says Hide extensions for known file types make sure you untick it. Now you can see file extensions.

Files and Extensions

All files have a name and usually have an extension that gives a clue as to the type of file and its purpose.

For instance asteroids.c is a C source code file that we'll be working on. The full file name is asteroids.c and the file extension is .c. Text files often got a .txt extension.

For files, extensions are important because if you double-click on a file Windows will run a program depending on the file extension. When you double click a .exe file, Windows runs it. If you double click a .txt file Windows opens it in Notepad.

Folders don't have extensions though they can have full stops in their name.

File Explorer

This is what File Explorer looks like.

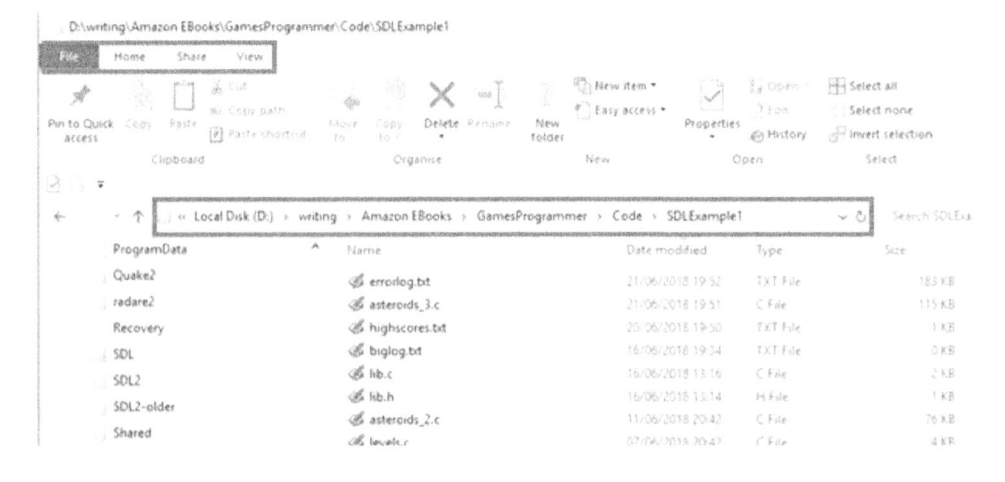

I've highlighted the top menu (File Home Share View) mentioned earlier. This has folders on the left and files on the right. Halfway down I've highlighted the address bar showing the full path to the folder with files shown on the right. In that folder you can see files with .c, .h and .txt extensions.

Every computer program is a collection of one or more files in a folder. All program files have a name and an extension like .exe or .dll. If it's a .exe then you can run it. If it's a .dll then it belongs to a .exe. A .dll file is a library and you can't run it at all. The code in that .dll library is used by a .exe when you run it.

Chapter 4. Bytes and Bobs and some Maths

In this chapter, I'll show some of the technical knowledge that you will need to program in C. Don't worry- there's not that much to learn!

In digital electronics, the memory (RAM and ROM) is made up of many little switches that are either on or off. Sometimes we use false and true or give them a numeric value such as 0 for false and 1 for true.

Internally the chips and circuits use different voltages such as 1V, 3.3V, 5V and 12V. You'll find some or most of those chips inside your computer but in software we're really only interested in the two false/true values that are 0 and 1 in C.

> Bit – Short for binary digit and is either 0 or 1.

We call such a switch by the name **bit**, short for binary digit. Because of the way memory chips are designed we don't access bits individually. Instead they are grouped in multiples of eight and we call each group of 8 bits a **byte**.

A byte has 8 bits side by side. Each bit has two values so a byte can have 2 x 2 x 2 x 2 x 2 x 2 x 2 x 2 = 256 different values. Those values are the complete range of numbers between 0 and 255.

> Byte – Eight bits

A Little bit of Math(s)

In maths (that's what British people call math), you might remember that a decimal number like 145 is made up of 1 x 100 + 4 x 10 + 5. Each position to the left is 10 times bigger.

100x	10x	1	Value
1	4	5	=145

It's the same in Base 2 (aka binary) - each position to the left is 2 times more.

So 145 in decimal looks like this: 10010001 in base 2:

128x	64x	32x	16x	8x	4x	2x	1x	Value
1	0	0	1	0	0	0	1	=145

Just add the number at the top for each bit's value. So 10010001 in decimal = 128 + 16 + 1 = 145.

Binary is cumbersome to work with so instead of base 2, it's common to work in base 16. This is called hexadecimal.

> Hexadecimal = Base 16

Four bits can hold 16 values (2 x 2 x 2 x 2 = 16). So in four bits we can represent any of the 16 values from 0 to 15. Those four bits make up a hexadecimal digit.

> Byte = 2 Hexadecimal digits e.g. F6

In hexadecimal for decimal values 0-9, we just use 0-9 but for decimal values 10-15 we use A-F in hexadecimal. Each byte is 8 bits and can be expressed as two hexadecimal digits.

Here are those values laid out side by side in decimal and hexadecimal.

Decimal	Hexadecimal	Decimal	Hexadecimal
0	0	8	8
1	1	9	9
2	2	10	A
3	3	11	B
4	4	12	C
5	5	13	D
6	6	14	E
7	7	15	F

The case of hexadecimal digits A-F isn't important so F4 and f4 means the same value = 244 in decimal.

Converting decimal 145 into binary gives 10010001; we can also convert it into two hexadecimal digits.

The top four bits are 1001, The bottom four bits are 0001.

8	4	2	1	Value
x	x	x	x	
1	0	0	1	=9

8	4	2	1	Value
x	x	x	x	
0	0	0	1	=1

So 145 in decimal = 91 in base 16 = 10010001 in binary.

In hexadecimal each position to the left of a digit is 16 times larger. So to convert a byte value in hexadecimal to decimal multiply the left digit by 16 and add the right digit.

0E = 14 (0 x 16 + 14)
21 = 33 (2 x 16 + 1)
F0 = 240 (15 x 16 + 0)
FF = 255 (15 x 16 + 15)

In C code, hexadecimal numbers have a prefix 0x so if you see **0xF0** you know it means 240 in decimal. You can use these as you wish and don't forget: single digits like 9 just mean 9 in both decimal and hexadecimal.

With numbers like 10 you need to know whether it's decimal 10 (= hexadecimal A) or hexadecimal 10 (=16 in decimal). For most C programming you won't need hexadecimal but there 's just a few times when you will.

Octal

C also supports another base - 8, or Octal as it's known. If you see a number that starts with a 0 and I promise you won't in this eBook after this chapter, it means it's a base 8 number. Every digit to the left is 8 times larger.

```
035 = 3 * 8 + 5 = 29 decimal
077 = 7 * 8 + 7 = 63 decimal
```

I just mention it because you might see it elsewhere and it lets me tell the classic C programming joke.

Q. Why do C programmers get confused between Halloween and Christmas Day?

A. Because Oct 31 = Dec 25.

31 in Octal (strictly it should be 031 but hey it's a joke) has a value = 8 x 3 + 1 which is 25 in decimal. Now forget I ever mentioned octal. *You will never need it.*

Files are bytes too!

A byte is either in RAM - remember that's main memory, or exists on disk in a file.

To give a sense of proportion. A typical paperback novel is maybe 60,000 to 70,000 words, roughly 300,000 bytes. If your computer has 4 GB (Gigabytes) of RAM. It can hold over 13,000 novels in memory at the same time.

More about Bytes

We can use byte size (8 bit) numbers for many calculations but we will need larger numbers, i.e. larger than 255. For example screen sizes such as 1920 x 1048. Two bytes together (16 bits) can hold 256 x 256 values = 65,536.

In hexadecimal a 16-bit number is four digits ranging from 0x0000 to 0xFFFF.

Even this can be too small so four bytes = 32 bits and 256 x 256 x 256 x 256 = 4,294,967,296 values. We often need negative numbers so a 32 bit number can be treated as either

- Unsigned with a range of values 0..4,294,967,295
- Signed with a range of values -2,147,483,648 .. 2,147,483,647.

Don't worry about signed/unsigned for now. Most of the time we'll use signed numbers, but **never ever mix unsigned and signed numbers**.

It's such a bad practice that it's sure to accelerate the heat death of the universe by a million years. Ok, that's maybe a slight exaggeration.

What's a signed number in hexadecimal?

It doesn't exist. The concept of negative numbers only applies in decimal. The largest unsigned 32 bit number is 4,294,967,295. In hexadecimal that's 0xFFFFFFFF. That is also the same as -1 in a signed 32 bit number!

The computer works only in terms of on/off switches. A 32 bit number is just 32 switches side by side, or 4 bytes in memory. Whether the bit pattern 11111111 11111111 11111111 11111111 is treated as -1 or 4,294,967,295 is entirely up to your program and if it is using signed or unsigned numbers.

Generally stick to using signed numbers and **never ever mix them with signed numbers in the same program.** You'll just get confusing results.

Multiple Byte numbers

In C, we store numbers in multiples of eight-bit sizes. Remember eight-bits = one byte. Most common are 4, 8 and sometimes 16 bytes.

If a byte in RAM holds the hexadecimal value 0x41, we know that is decimal 65 (4 x 16 + 1= 65), but if we are storing text, it also means the character A instead. To the computer it's just 8 electrical switches with the switch (i.e. binary) pattern 01000001. It's what we do with that value that matters.

For a short change from all this heavy math(s) stuff, we'll now look at a simple C program. We won't run it but I just want you to see what C looks like.

In the next chapter we'll look at our first C program.

Chapter 5. Hello World

It's a tradition to start with a Hello World program. Yes a bit cheesy but we'll give it a go.

Below is a Hello World program in C. You write C programs in a form of English that a C compiler can read and translate it into instructions that the computer can run.

I haven't shown you a C compiler yet so you can't compile or run the program. A C compiler converts your C program into instructions that the CPU can run.

CPUs do not understand English or even C source code, but once the C compiler translates it, the CPU can then run the compiled code or machine code as it's usually called.

Listing of Hello World

```
#include <stdio.h>
main( )
{
    printf("hello world\n");
}
```

There are two parts to this. This is the first.

#include <stdio.h>. It looks like gobbledegook but it tells the compiler that you wish to include code from a library called stdio.

The .h extension is because every C library has a header file with a .h extension.

A C library also includes code that's been compiled and the compiler adds that precompiled code into your application and then outputs a single exe. You can write your own libraries once you get familiar with C. It's a useful way of splitting a program into smaller parts.

If your program has to output text to a command line window (more on this is a moment), it must use stdio. It's a library that lets your program read input from the keyboard and output to the screen. As we're outputting Hello World on the screen we need stdio.

This is the second part.

main(). Every C program has one. It tells the compiler that this is the point where the program starts running from. Technically the OS (Windows) begins executing the code between the { } (known as curly brackets or curly braces) in the main().

The reason for the () in main is because main is a function and I'll explain functions later. For now, just know that a function is a way of grouping C code statements together as one statement that you can call from different places in your program.

Command Line Window?

If you've ever watched a film with hackers, you'll know that they don't use a mouse but instead type in commands.

Back before Windows and Mac OS came along, the only way to use a computer then was to type in commands and this can still be very useful and not just when you are hacking!

Three three OS (Windows, Mac and Linux) still have command lines though only Windows calls them that; the others call them terminal windows or just terminals.

To open a command line, hold the Windows key and Press R. The Windows key is usually the one with 2 x 2 slanted rectangles on the bottom row of the keyboard between the Ctrl and Alt keys. It looks like this on the left....

You should see a popup Window with the title Run and a text box to the right of the word Open.

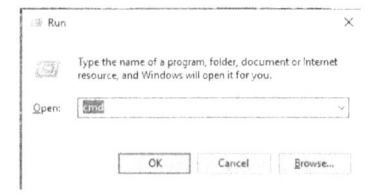

Type in cmd and press the Enter key or click the OK button.

Now a command line window will open and your quest to be a "leet hacker" begins. Ok, so I made the last bit up but who knows?

This is a cmd window in Windows.

Now type in

echo hello world

Then press the enter key and you should see something like this, also shown on the image to the left.

C:\Users\David>echo Hello World

Hello World

It's what you would see if you had compiled your C Hello World program and run it. As you can't do that yet, we'd better get you setup with a decent C compiler and we'll do that in the next chapter.

Chapter 6. Installing Visual Studio Community Edition

Microsoft have an excellent development system called Visual Studio. Note you need to be running Windows 7 Service Pack 1 or Windows 10 to install it.

It's available in several editions including Community (which is free), Professional and Enterprise. The current version is the 2017 one and is available here. If you are reading this in the future then you may find a different numbered version but anything you learn in this EBook will still apply.

Downloading Files

Windows 10 has a special protection system for files you download from the internet.

Find the file using File Manager or your browser. If you use Chrome, the three vertical dots on the right hand side popup a menu with Downloads as in the image below.

Click that and you'll see the files you have recently downloaded.

Click the relevant Show in Folder and it will open Windows File Explorer highlighting the downloaded file which should be called **vs_community.exe**.

Now right click on it and click properties right at the bottom of the popup menu. This will open a properties Window. At the bottom of the first Tab (General) you might see a security warning and an Unblock tick box. Just tick that to allow Windows to let you access it. If there's no unblock then you are free to run it.

Run **vs_community.exe** to start installing. After asking you, it will take a while depending on your internet download speed. You'll probably have enough time for a coffee, a three-course meal or a two week cruise depending on your internet speed.

Once installed, run the installer again anytime to add or remove features. On the Start menu look for **Visual Studio Installer**. When run it shows what you have installed and you can click Update (if a button shows that) to update it to the latest version.

You can also click the Modify button to go to the screen showing the different Workloads. For this course the only one you need is "**Desktop Development with C++**". The second one down on the left.

After installation finishes, look in your start menu by clicking the Start button then scroll down to Visual Studio 2017. You will see two entries, one a folder and the other a purple icon. Click the purple icon and Visual Studio will run.

You may have to register with Microsoft when you first run it but it's free so don't worry.

With Visual Studio open you'll see a Purple icon on the Taskbar at the bottom of your screen. If you right click on the icon you get a popup menu and one of the options is Pin to taskbar. Click that and you'll get a permanent shortcut on the taskbar. It looks like this.

You are now ready to begin creating a project and then you'll be able to write code, save it, edit it, compile it and run it. In Chapter 7 I'll show you how to setup a project and run Hello World for real.

Projects

Most programs are complex enough that you need several files. Visual Studio works by letting you create a project for each application and you can then add source code files to it, as well as graphics and sound files if you wish.

In the asteroids game, I'll just be mostly having source code files in the project. The graphics and sound files will be loaded from disk at runtime.

Game Source Code

Chapter 50 tells you how to get the complete sources, images etc. It includes all the source examples that you need when learning C as well as the game source code.

In the next chapter we'll start on the first project.

Chapter 7. Our first project

When Visual Studio opens, it usually starts on the Start Page. This shows you recently opened projects and lets you do New Project. No prizes for guessing that that creates a new project.

I prefer to do that from the File menu. Click File then move the Cursor to New and you'll see a submenu popup with Project at the top; I've highlighted it in red. Click that.

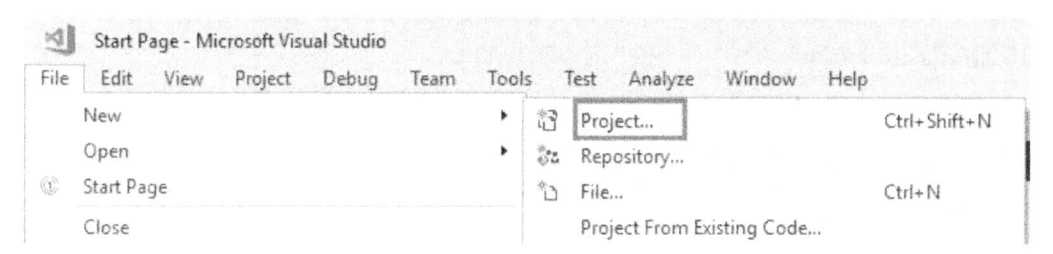

Start Page - Microsoft Visual Studio										
File	Edit	View	Project	Debug	Team	Tools	Test	Analyze	Window	Help
New				▶		Project...				Ctrl+Shift+N
Open				▶		Repository...				
Start Page						File...				Ctrl+N
Close						Project From Existing Code...				

You should now see a New Project form. On the left look under Installed for Visual C++. Click that and you should see on the right a menu showing Windows Console Application, Windows Desktop Application and Empty Project.

We'll be creating Windows Console Application for the 30 or so example applications. C doesn't include any graphics, you need 3rd party libraries for that.

Click on Windows Console Application to select it. Towards the bottom of the form Type in HelloWorld for the name. You should see Solution name say HelloWorld and make sure the Create Directory for solution is checked.

These are all highlighted in the next picture.

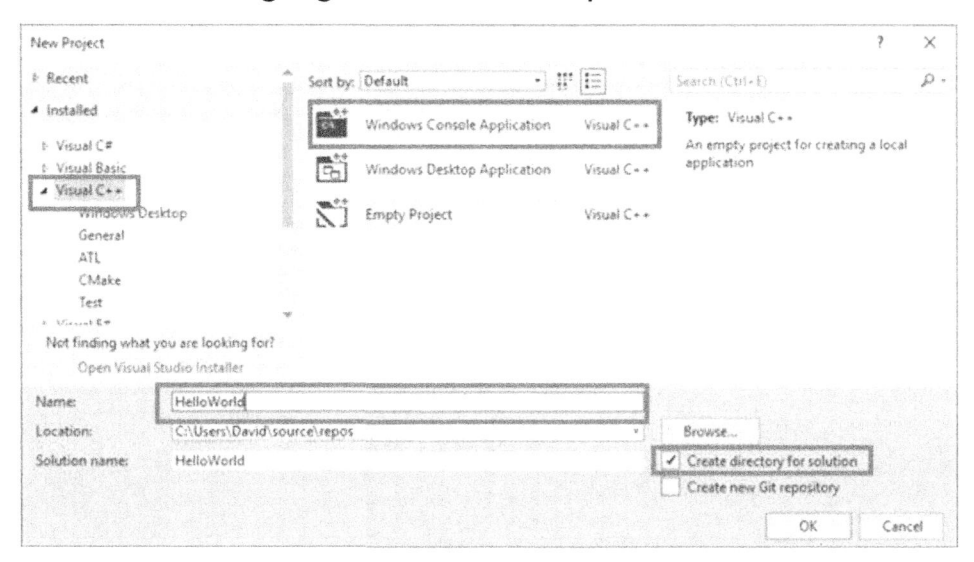

This create a default C++ application **not C**, so do these.

1. Double click HelloWorld.cpp in the right hand pane below.
2. Select the HelloWorld source code listed in chapter 5 and paste it or just type it in. It should look a bit like this.

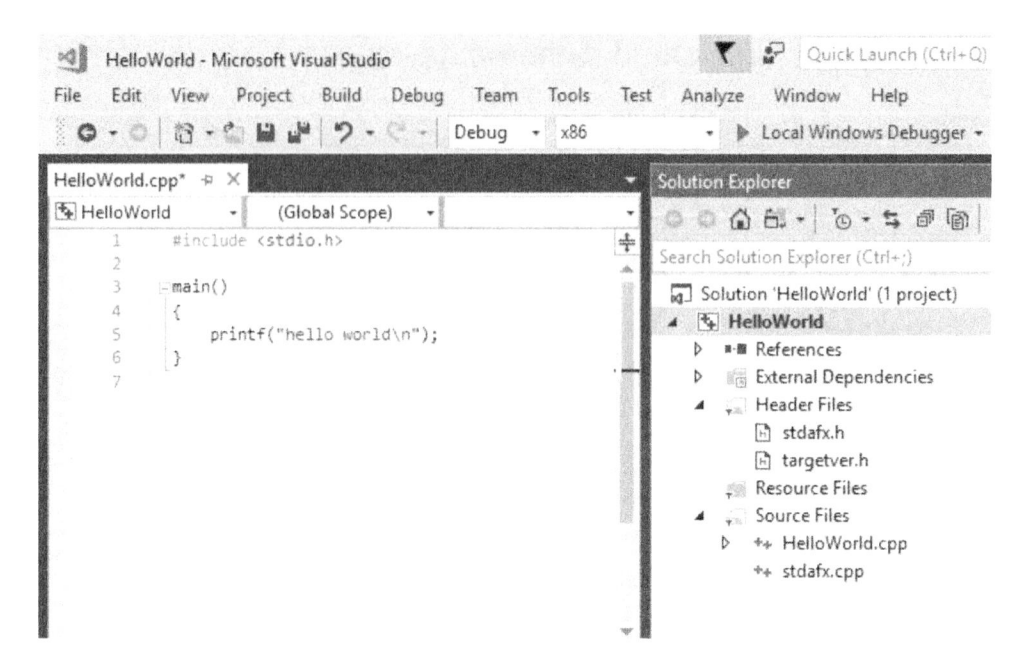

Once you've done that, you'll see a * after the **HelloWorld.cpp** text in the tab. That means your file isn't saved, so either click the Save button icon or hit Ctrl-s by holding the Ctrl key (bottom left on most keyboards) and pressing s at the same time. Once it's saved the * will vanish.

The project has three files that we do not need. In the Solution Explorer window on the right of the **HelloWorld.cpp** window, it lists the project files. While holding the Ctrl key down click once on these files (**stadafx.h**, **targetver.h** and **stdafx.cpp**) but not **HelloWorld.cpp**.

Now right click on any of the selected files and you should see a popup menu window.

Click Remove and on the Window that appears giving you Remove, Delete and Cancel buttons. We'll never need those files so click the Delete button.

Next right click on **HelloWorld.cpp** and click rename. Remove the pp from the **HelloWorld.cpp** and press enter. You'll see the Solution Explorer and the Edit Window tab both change to **HelloWorld.c**. If there's a * save the file.

Now your solution explorer should look a bit like this:

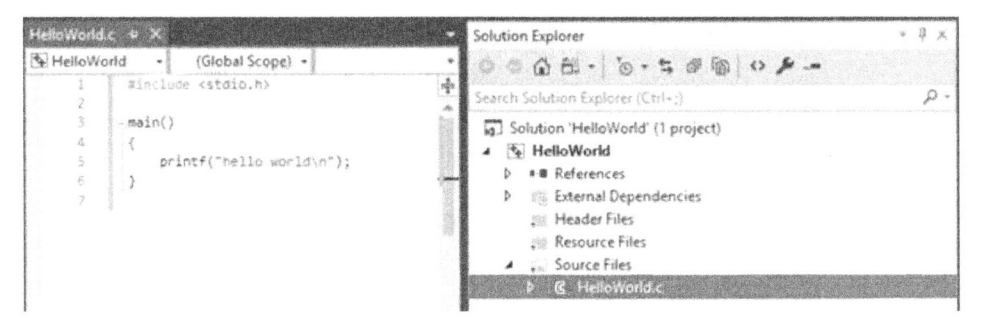

You must make these changes to the Project Options. Click Project on the Top menu and at the bottom of the popup menu that appears click Properties. A Window titled **HelloWorld.c** Property pages will appear. Do the following:

- Where it says Configuration:, click the Pulldown to the right and change **Active(Debug)** to **All Configurations**.
- Change the Platform: pulldown to **Win32**.
- Look down the Configuration Properties for C/C++ and click on **Precompiled Headers**. On the right hand side where it says **Use (/Yu)** click on it and change it to **Not Using Precompiled Headers**.
- Click Apply at the bottom of the Property Pages then Ok. The Window will close.

Open the property pages again and make sure the highlighted controls have these values.

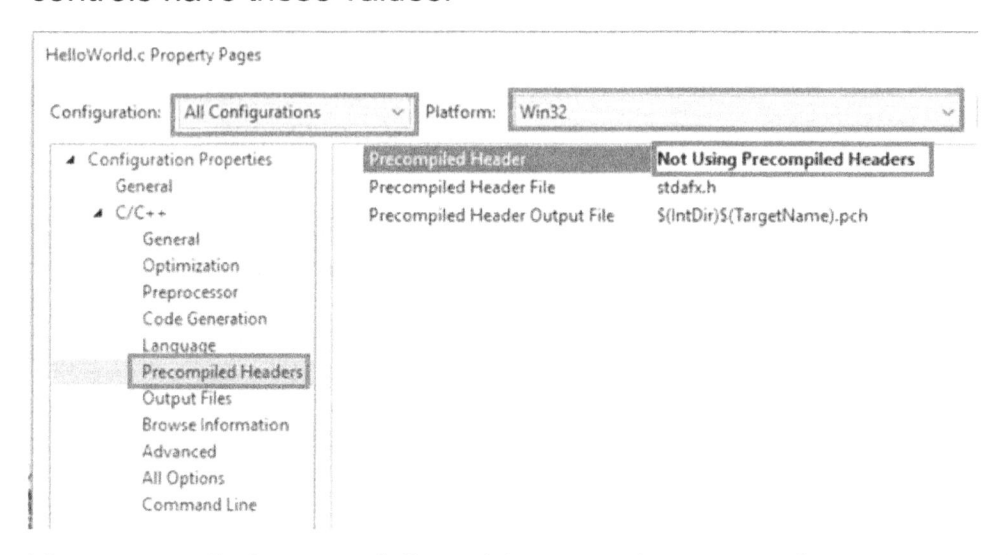

```
HelloWorld.c Property Pages

Configuration: All Configurations      Platform: Win32

▲ Configuration Properties        Precompiled Header            Not Using Precompiled Headers
    General                       Precompiled Header File       stdafx.h
  ▲ C/C++                         Precompiled Header Output File  $(IntDir)$(TargetName).pch
      General
      Optimization
      Preprocessor
      Code Generation
      Language
      Precompiled Headers
      Output Files
      Browse Information
      Advanced
      All Options
      Command Line
```

You generally have to follow this procedure once for each new C project as Microsoft defaults projects to C++.

After making these changes **you can compile and link your C program by pressing the F6 button**.

> To compile your program press the F6 key

It will think, whirr and then (hopefully) output the following:

1>------ Build started: Project: HelloWorld, Configuration: Debug Win32 ------

1>HelloWorld.c
1>HelloWorld.vcxproj ->
C:\Users\David\source\repos\HelloWorld\Debug\HelloWorld.exe
========== **Build: 1 succeeded**, 0 failed, 0 up-to-date, 0 skipped ==========

The 3rd line will vary because the paths will be different. What is important is the fourth line. Build: 1 succeeded etc.

If that doesn't happen, check your program listing against Chapter 5. Make any changes then hit F6 to build. If your files isn't saved, F6 will also save it before compiling.

Assuming you were successful press ctrl-F5 and your program will run. It should open a command line window and you should see this text.

hello world

Press any key to continue . . .

Result! You've built and run your first C program. One small step for mankind, one big step for you!

Some notes on this chapter.

I mentioned link in 'compile and link'. Compiling turns HelloWorld.c into HelloWorld.obj, into what is called an object file. You will probably never see this.

To produce an executable (the HelloWorld.exe), after the compiler has compiled, another program called a Linker is run and takes all the object files: HelloWorld.obj plus the stdio code and links them all together with some boilerplate code (you will never see this) into the HelloWorld.exe.

Generally linking is an automatic part of compiling so you don't need to worry about it too much.

If you press F5 instead of Ctrl-F5, the program will run, you'll see the window open but it will then immediately finish and close.

Also after making a change to the program, pressing Ctrl-F5 will save it out, do the compilation and if it works run it. The first time you do this, it will ask if you want to run it but you can tick a checkbox so it doesn't ask in future.

Printing on Multiple Lines

Referring back to the HelloWorld listing in chapter 5. After the text hello World you'll see a \n. Try changing the text in the printf() to this:

"hello world\nOn a New line\n"

The program listing should now look like this.

```
#include <stdio.h>
int main()
{
   printf("hello world\nOn a new line\n");
}
```

Run it and it will now output that text on two lines. The \n inside a string starts printing on the next line.

That was a major bit of learning. We've now got a large part of our tools in place, so the next few chapters will now look at C. Well done!

Chapter 8. Variables in C.

Most programming involves data, whether counting it, manipulating it or doing all sorts of things to it.

There might be 37 asteroids on screen at a given moment and we need to hold that number somewhere. Each asteroid faces in one of 24 directions. and we need to keep that information along with its speed.

Remember I said computers have RAM? When we run a program Windows loads the program into RAM and runs it starting at main().

We also use RAM for holding the program's data which is often numbers and text. We do this by giving each piece of data a name and we use that in the program. These are known as variables because their content can vary.

As well as a name we need to say what kind of data we are going to store and we do this by choosing a type. The C compiler know how much RAM each type will occupy and it can allocate the correct number of bytes to hold all variables.

We do this in a C program by declaring a variable of a given type and giving it a name. There are two ways of declaring a variable:

Type Name;
Type Name = Initial Value;
For example

int numAsteroids= 37;
int direction;
float total = 0.0f;
unsigned int counter;

Don't worry about **float** or 0.0f for now. I will explain these later. **Float** is a type of variable that holds numbers with decimal points.

The first declaration declares a 32 bit **int** variable called numAsteroids and gives it a value of 37.

The **int** is the type. It's always first in a declaration. It tells the compiler to allocate four bytes to hold an **int** and the type will be signed.

If you put **unsigned** in front of **int**, it will be unsigned i.e. only zero or positive values. The other types that we'll come across are **float**, **double** and **char**. More on those later.

Don't forget to end the declaration with a semi-colon ; it separates statements. You can put them on the same line like this below but it's harder to read so please don't!

int numAsteroids= 37; int direction;

What is a Variable?

It's a name for a place to hold data.

When a program runs, the operating system grabs some of the computer's RAM to hold all of the variables. If any variable has an initial value then those are placed there.

Note that the initial value is optional. If you declare it without an initial value, it will just use what was in memory already.

Because of the way Windows works, every time you run the program it will load it into a different location in RAM. The addresses allocated for variables also vary on each run.

You have to declare a variable before you use it, or the compiler gets confused and you get a **identifier 'variable name' is undefined** compile error. You have to fix all compile errors or the compiler won't generate any code and your program won't run.

Numeric types for variables

We'll start with numeric types. The most common type is **int** which is a signed 32 bit number with no decimal part. It can hold numbers from -2,147,483,648 to 2,147,483,647 and occupies 4 bytes of RAM when the program runs.

So the following lines declare two **int** variables count and height.

```
int count = 0;
int height;
```

Other types include

- **short** - 16 bit. Numbers from -32768 to 32767.
- **long** - Same as int on Windows (32 bit) but on Linux may be a different size.
- **long long** - 64 bit.

```
short int littlevariable=10;
long long bignumber = 1000000000000000;
unsigned long long biggernumber = 10000000000000000;
```

In the examples folder there's a file **declarations.c** which contains a number of declarations.

How big are variables of a specified type?

By big, I mean how many bytes do variables of the various types occupy in RAM when the program runs?

This short C program uses printf() again and a built-in function called sizeof() to output the size of the **int, float, double, short, long** and **long long** types.

```
#include <stdio.h>
int main()
{
  printf("Size of char = %d\n", sizeof(char));
  printf("Size of short = %d\n", sizeof(short));
  printf("Size of int = %d\n", sizeof(int));
  printf("Size of long = %d\n", sizeof(long));
  printf("Size of long long = %d\n", sizeof(long long));
  printf("Size of float = %d\n", sizeof(float));
  printf("Size of double = %d\n", sizeof(double));
  return 0;
}
```

Whe you run it, the output is

Size of char = 1
Size of short = 2
Size of int = 4
Size of long = 4
Size of long long = 8
Size of float = 4
Size of double = 8

These sizes are in bytes so multiply by 8 to get the number of bits.

The %d in the printf is a placeholder and tells the compiler where the output string will have an **int** variable. It needs a corresponding value to print and that's what the sizeof() in each line provides.

In games programming we won't use printf to output text but we'll use it for now while you are learning.

Note. Short, **int** and **long long** are all integer types; they just vary in size.

Snippets

Rather than you typing the whole program, save out the code below and type in the code snippet where the **// snippets go here** is. The // means it's a comment. You can leave it in with the snippet code or remove it. It won't affect compilation. Comments are just notes left in the code.

You can add // comments anywhere and I encourage you do so, to add extra meaning to your program that isn't always obvious from the code itself. You'll see the game sources have lots of comments.

```
#include <stdio.h>
int main()
{
    // snippets go here
    return 0;
}
```

Unsigned types

Remember variables are signed, i.e. they can be negative like -5. We can also hold unsigned versions of these types by putting the word unsigned in front. Unsigned only hold 0 or positive numbers.

unsigned int total = 2000;

The lowest value that an **unsigned int** can hold is 0, the highest is 4,294,967,295. An **unsigned int** is the same size as a signed **int**.

As a rule, you should never mix unsigned variables and signed. Remember **int, short, long** etc are signed numbers and I've managed by just using them for several years, and I have never needed unsigned variables.

Try this short snippet.

unsigned int ui = 4294967294;
int i = ui;
printf("Value of i = %d", i);

What value do you think it prints for i? The answer is -2. Confusing isn't it! It's best practice not to mix them. The reason for the -2? Go reread What's a signed number in hexadecimal.

Floating Point variables

C includes two types for numbers with a decimal point like 0.5. The two types are **float** and **double**. **Float** variables take up 4 bytes and provide 6-7 digits after the decimal point while **double** take up 8 bytes but have a bigger range and 15-16 digits after the decimal point.

Which type you use depends on what type of data you want to hold. If you were measuring temperature then a **float** would do as you would only need 1 or 2 decimal places. For a highly accurate measurement, to many decimal places you probably use a **double**.

This snippet shows the respective sizes of **floats** and **doubles**.

```
printf("Size of float = %d\n", sizeof(float));
printf("Size of double = %d\n", sizeof(double));
```

As usual with snippets just copy the text and paste the text between { and } in the **short, long** etc example with it.

When you run it, it should output:

```
Size of float = 4
Size of double = 8
```

So an **int** and a **float** both occupy four bytes. As far as the CPU is concerned these are just 4 bytes in RAM. It's what we do with the variables that gives them meaning.

To print a **float** or **double** variable, you need to use %f instead of %d which is for integer variables. If you run this snippet.

```
float pi = 3.141592653589793f;
printf("Value of pi = %16.15f\n", pi);
```

You get this value output.

```
Value of pi = 3.141592741012573
```

41

After 7 decimal places the values vary a lot. That's the lack of precision because it's a **float**.

The %16.15f in the snippet below specifies the format with the 16 before the decimal point being the total width. The 15 after the decimal point is the number of digits after the decimal point to output.

Note the f at the end of the number when you declare it. That tells the compiler it's a **float**. For **doubles**, you use the letter l. That's a lower-case L not a 1.

If I change this snippet to double like this and run it.

```
double pi = 3.141592653589793l;
printf("Value of pi = %16.15f\n", pi);
```

That outputs "Value of pi = 3.141592653589793" which is exactly the defined value. That's the extra accuracy of doubles!

We'll use **floats** in the game though as we don't need this extra accuracy of **doubles** and using **float** variables saves memory. We're probably not saving that much memory but declaring variables with the correct size type is a good habit to learn.

In the next chapter we'll look at another type: **char**.

Chapter 9. Another type: char

Let's look at the **char** type first and then pointers. This snippet shows that chars occupy one byte each.

char a = 'A';
printf("Size of A = %d\n", sizeof(a));

That outputs **Size of A = 1**

If you wish to print a char the % format code is c.

printf("a = %c\n",a);

That outputs a = A.

However what do you think this prints?

printf("%d %c\n", 'A', 'A');

It prints 65 A. The integer value of 'A' is 65. Think of it that char types in C99 on Windows are a single byte int value.

int a = 'A';

Individual chars are useful in game programming. You want to know which key was pressed on the keyboard don't you?

C Strings

C strings are a bit quirky compared to strings in other programming languages. A string is an array of bytes that end with a zero value byte. This byte is added by the compiler so you rarely have to add it in code..

The quirkiness comes from the declaration of a C string. Here's a snippet that prints out Name = David.

```
char * name="David";
printf("Name = %s\n",name);
```

The type of a C-String is **char ***. When you see a * like this, it doesn't mean multiply but instead means pointer to a char.

Now it's too early in this course to fully explain a pointer so I'll give you a quick intro. and we'll return to them in chapter 19.

What is a Pointer variable?

A pointer variable doesn't hold a variable's value, it holds the address (in RAM) where the value is stored. Let me explain how it works with char * name= "David".

Variables are usually lumped together in one place. Say they are at address 5000. Think of computer memory (RAM and ROM) as like houses, each with its own numeric address.

Address 5,000 is a pointer that holds the address of the six characters that make up "David" - five letters plus a terminating 0 byte.

Let's say it's at address 30000 and occupies six successive bytes with one character in each byte at addresses 30000 - 30005. It looks like this.

30000 D	30001 a	30002 v
30003 i	30004 d	30005 0

Now let's say our pointer variable (we'll call it name- all variables have a name) is four bytes long at addresses 5000-5003. These four bytes hold the address of data i.e. the value 30000. If you convert 30000 into hexadecimal, the value is 00007530.

4096 x	256 x	16x	1 x
7	5	3	0

Remember (7 * 4096) + (5 * 256) + (3 * 16) = 30000.

On modern PCs, multi-byte numbers are stored in "Little Endian format". This is the reverse order so the four byte values (0, 3, 5 and 7) are stored in successive addresses like this.

5000 0
5001 3
5002 5
5003 7

When we do printf("Name=%s\n",name); the compiler generates code that fetches the four byte address name from locations 5000-5003. That contains the value 30000.

The code now reads successive characters from address 30000 onwards and prints each character until it reaches the 0 at address 30005.

Just as %c is the printf format string for char type variables %s is used for c-strings.

We use a few strings in the game, so you do need to know about them.

Just remember, when you use a pointer, there are two separate things. One is the pointer, occupying four bytes and holding the address of the variable elsewhere in memory.

It's like going to a numbered pigeonhole. using the example earlier, it's pigeonhole 5000. Instead of having our data there, it has a sign there saying "the number is in pigeonhole 30000". It really is as simple as that!

In the next chapter we'll look at some simple C code.

Chapter 10. A little Bit of C code

Now that we've seen declarations of variables, we'll write a bit of code to do math(s). Here's a longer snippet. It's in the examples folder as calc1.c.

```c
int a = 200;
int b = 150;
int c = a + b;
int d = a - b;
int e = a * b;
float f = (float)a / b;
printf("a = %d b= %d c = %d d = %d e = %d f= %f\n", a, b, c, d, e, f);
```

You could probably figure out the calculated values of c, d, e and f. Here * means multiply not a pointer. This outputs.

a = 200 b= 150 c = 350 d = 50 e = 30000 f= 1.333333

You might be wondering about the (float) in the **float** f line. It's called a cast and tells the compiler to perform a / b as a **float** instead of **int**. If you divide 200 by 150 and store the result in an **int** variable, you get 1 not 1.333333 because you need a **float** to hold 1.333333.

If you remove the (**float**) so it looks like this

```c
float f = a / b;
```

Then run it you'll see it now outputs f = 1.000000 because 150 goes into 200 once and there's no fractional part with **ints**.

More Code

Here is an if-else statement to compare a and b and output which is biggest.

The if statement evaluates the expression in brackets (a > b) and if true it does the next statement. If there is an else and the if expression is false, it does the statement in the else braces {}.

```c
int a = 200;
int b = 150;
if (a > b) {
   printf("a is bigger than b\n");
}
else {
   printf("b is bigger than a\n");
}
```

As you'd expect it prints "a is bigger than b".

Now part of programming is figuring out when code is not correct. That snippet of code has a bug in it. Can you see it?

If you change b to be bigger than a, it will correctly print "b is bigger than a". But change b to be the same as a and it will incorrectly print "b is bigger than a".

We must change it to see if a is the same as b, like this.

```c
int a = 200;
int b = 200;
if (a > b) {
   printf("a is bigger than b\n");
}
else if (b > a) {
   printf("b is bigger than a\n");
}
```

```
else {
    printf("b is equal to a\n");
}
```

> (a == b) is true if a equals b

To test if two variables are equal you have to use == and to test they are not the same use !=.

> (a != b) is true if a doesn't equal b

Here I've done two tests but I didn't use else which would have saved me from needing the second test.

```
int a = 200;
int b = 200;
if (a == b) {
    printf("a equals b\n");
}
if (a != b ) {
    printf("a does not equal b\n");
}
```

So if with or without an else is quite flexible.

Programming Mistakes in C

Let me warn you about some programming mistakes that you will inevitably make. Everyone makes them!

Testing for equality but using = instead of ==.
When run, this says "a equals b" which is obviously wrong.

```
int a = 200;
```

```
int b = 150;
if (a = b) {
    printf("a equals b\n");
}
if (a != b ) {
    printf("a does not equal b\n");
}
```

Unfortunately C allows **if (a = b)** as well as **if (a== b)**. So a = b copies b's value into a, and evaluates it (150) as true.

Here's another surprise. If you change the 2nd line to int b = 0, what will it print?

Answer, nothing at all.

It also copies b's value into a, but as b is now 0 the value of (0) is false. C treats 0 as false and any non-zero value as true.

So if your code behaves oddly look out for **=** that should be **==**.

Note. The bit after the if is called an expression and must always be in brackets. so **if a == b** is not allowed, it must be **if (a == b)**.

TIP

To avoid the **if (a = 8)** when it should be **if (a==8)**, try writing it backwards as **if (8 == a)** instead of **if (a == 8)**.

The compiler will certainly object to **if (8 = a)** which is good instead of **if (a = 8)** which is bad.

In the next chapter, I'll take a closer look at Visual Studio and show you some ways to do things better.

Chapter 11. A Quick Overview of Visual Studio

Visual Studio lets you create projects, configure them, compile and then debug your code. It has many useful features that make editing easier.

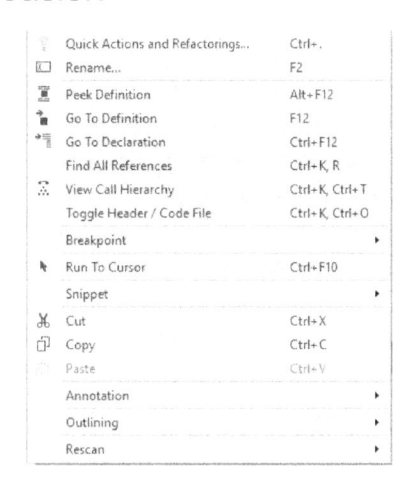

For example if you right click on a function- such as printf(), a popup menu appears and when you click **Go to Definition** it takes you to the source code of printf().

That's not particularly useful but when you have a lot of functions, it makes navigating them much easier. Plus you can right-click click on a function and then click Find All References. That produces a clickable list of all places in your project with calls to that function.

You can also create a bookmark on lines of interest and navigate quickly between bookmarks.

You can search in a local file, just in selected text or through every file in your project.

Just above the edit window, when you have a file being edited you should see three sections. The first is to the project if you have multiple projects in a solution. We don't so you can ignore that.

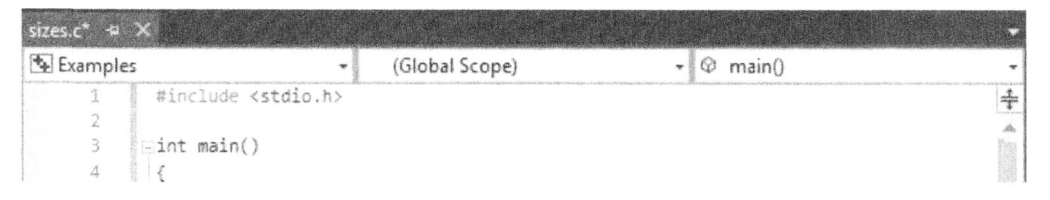

```
sizes.c*
Examples                    (Global Scope)              main()
    1    #include <stdio.h>
    2
    3    int main()
    4    {
```

The second section (Global Scope) is a pulldown to global variables, i.e. those declared outside of any function, select something from the list and the editor will jump to its declaration.

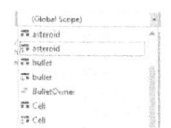

The first two entries say asteroid but have different icons. The first icon which is a flat line with two squares beneath jumps to the declaration of the asteroid struct.

The second icon has a little arrow instead of the left square and this jumps to where the asteroids array is declared.

The third section is an alphabetic list of all functions. Now I usually have all functions start with a capital letter but I found three that didn't and these ended up at the end of the list. Select a function name and it will jump to that function.

- AddAlienShip()
- AddAsteroid(int sizeindex)
- AddExplosion(int x, int y)
- AddObjectToCells(pfirstpart objectptr)
- AddPointerToCell(int x, int y, pfirstpart objectptr)
- AddTextSpriteAt(char * value, int x, int y, int textfactor)
- AddTextSpriteInt(int value, int y, int textfactor)
- AddTextSpriteString(char * value, int y, int textfactor)
- AdjustShield()
- AlienHitOwnBullet(pfirstpart object1, pfirstpart object2)
- AllObjectsDestroyed()

Jumping backwards and forwards.

By default you should have the Standard toolbar visible. If you can't see the Standard Toolbar click anywhere blank on the top section (the one that has the File Edit View Menu). You should see a popup list of toolbars. Tick the ones you want, and make sure Standard is ticked.

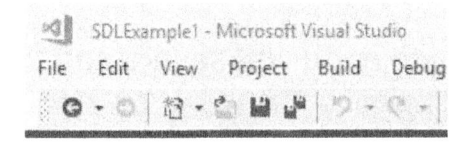

This is normally the first toolbar on the line below under the File menu. It has several icons but only the first two are important.

If you've jumped somewhere using a bookmark or a pull down of functions/variables then you'll see a back arrow visible on the standard Toolbar.

Click this back arrow and it will return you to the point in the editor where you were before your last jump. It keeps a history so when you've jumped to a few places, you'll be able to jump backwards or forwards via the forward arrow.

Finally when you are on a function call, and you wish to see the definition you can get there in two other ways. Right click on it and in the popup menu you'll see **Peek Definition** and **Go to Definition**.

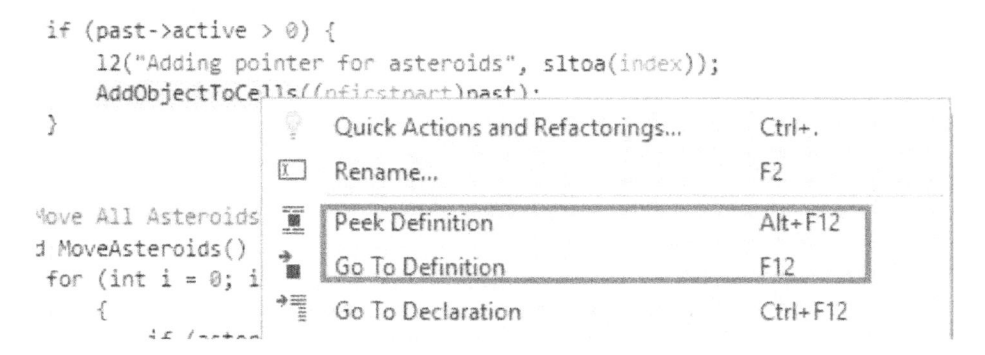

```
if (past->active > 0) {
    l2("Adding pointer for asteroids", sltoa(index));
    AddObjectToCells((nfirstpart)past);
}
```

	Quick Actions and Refactorings...	Ctrl+.
	Rename...	F2
	Peek Definition	Alt+F12
	Go To Definition	F12
	Go To Declaration	Ctrl+F12

Peek Definition opens up an edit Window in your edit window, so you can change the function. I've already mentioned **Go to Definition** that just jumps to the function declaration.

Alternatively with the mouse pointer over the function hold the control key down and you'll see it underline the function name. Now just click the mouse left button and you'll jump to the function's definition. Learning these ways of navigating your project will save you a lot of time when editing.

Adding or Removing files from a Solution

Visual Studio has two types of project. There's the normal project which compiles to a .exe or a .dll depending on what you set it up as.

But there's also a Solution which is a collection of projects. For what we're doing we'll use single-project solutions.

If you right-click on a source file in Solution Explorer, two of the options in the popup menu are **Exclude From Project** and **Remove**. Exclude is the safer, it just removes the file from the project but leaves it in the folder on disk.

Remove does pretty much the same but gives you the option of deleting the file as well. That's deleting a file on disk so be careful!

If you right-click on Source Files in Solution explorer the first option in the popup menu is **Add** and you can add a **New Item** or an **Existing Item**.

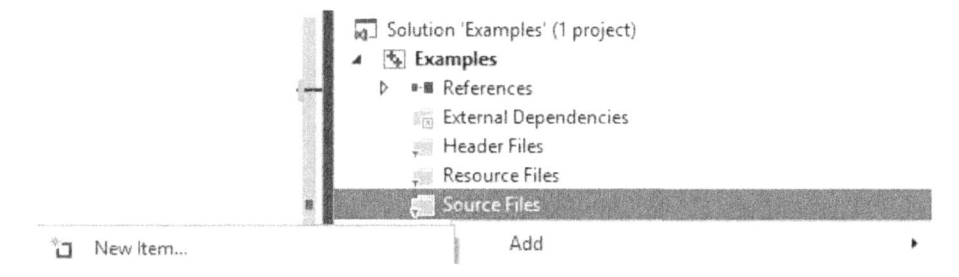

```
    Solution 'Examples' (1 project)
    ▲ 🔧 Examples
        ▷ ■■ References
            External Dependencies
            Header Files
            Resource Files
            Source Files
```

  ⁺🗋 New Item...   Add   ▸

It's a handy way of switching between files if you only want one source file in a project. If you want to add in say declarations.c but currently have calc1.c in the project then Exclude calc1.c and Add Existing item declarations.c.

Of course you can have multiple source files or header files in a project.

In the next chapter we'll take a look at array variables.

Chapter 12. Array variables

So far the variables we've declared have been single instances of ints, floats etc. These are known as scalar variables.

But very often it's handy to have an array of variables. An array is a variable with a name and fixed number of elements, all of the same type. To define an array you declare a variable with **[number]** on the end. For example:

int balloons[10];
float speeds[5];

Balloons is an array of ten ints and speed an array of five floats.

Working with arrays

I used the house analogy for memory locations earlier and arrays are similar.

Let's say you have ten cars. You want to hold their top speeds and engine sizes. Speed is stored to 1/10th MPH eg 170.8 so we need floats for that. For engine size, it ranges from 1600 to 5400 so int is a suitable type.

Here are the declarations.

#define NUMBERCARS 10
int engineCC[NUMBERCARS];
float topSpeed[NUMBERCARS];

Here I have introduced a new C language feature called #define. It lets you define some text that the compiler substitutes when it is compiling.

I've defined NUMB

#define – declares text to be substituted when compiling

ERCARS as being 10 and used it in the declarations because

we've got two arrays declared. Both have the same number of elements- 10. Now I could have just declared them like this:

int engineCC[10];
float topSpeed[10];

Numbers in code like this are called 'magic

> Magic Numbers – a number that should have a symbolic name but is in the code as a literal. E.g. 10

numbers'. It's far better to use names than magic numbers.

If you used a number in many places in your program and decided to change it then you'd have to manually find and change each one. It's less risky to change the #define value.

What if one of the 10s changed to 15 and you didn't notice? Code that assumed the two arrays had the same number of elements might crash because of the difference.

It's good practice to avoid magic numbers and use the #define value throughout your program. It makes it more readable; you can see what it is – NUMBER_CARS not just a number 10.

Accessing and using arrays

So now we have our two arrays, how do we use them? First we have to assign values. Now in C99, the version of C that we are using lets us initialize all values in one statement. Here's the full program. It's in the Examples folders as cars.c.

```
#include <stdio.h>
#define NUMBERCARS 10
int engineCC[NUMBERCARS] = {
1600,1800,2000,2400,2500,2800,3500,4000,4500,5400 };
float topSpeed[NUMBERCARS] = {
120.0f,132.6f,142.8f,150.5f,170.8f,173.2f,175.6f, 178.4f,181.8f, 188.7f };
```

```c
int main()
{
 int index = 4;
 printf("Car %d Engine CC = %d Top Speed = %6.2f\n",
    index, engineCC[index], topSpeed[index]);
 return 0;
}
```

Running this produces:

Car 4 Engine CC = 2500 Top Speed = 170.80

If you count the values for engineCC, you'll notice that 2500 is the 5th number, likewise for 170.8 in the topSpeed array. In C, the index i.e. the value in [brackets] starts from 0, not 1.

So the first value is engineCC is at index 0, i.e. engineCC[0] and is 1600. The last element index is 9 so topSpeed[9] is 188.7.

Counting from 0

This is a very important thing in C. Everything counts from 0 not 1. One or two other programming languages count from 1, but not C or C++ or most popular programming languages.

Here's a declaration of ten ints with the name values.

int values[10];

The first element in the array is values[0], the second values[1] and the last is values[9]. You'll get used to it eventually.

Multiple dimension arrays

The arrays we've looked at are single dimensions, sometimes known as a vector. We can have 2, 3 or as many dimensions as you like subject to limitations of memory.

For instance say you were using a char for a piece on a chess set. You might declare it like this.

char chessBoard[8][8];

That's a two dimension array. 8 rows of 8 columns, 64 values in total. The top left piece is chessboard[0][0] and the bottom right one is chessboard[7][7].

The most dimensions used in the asteroids game is three. That's for collision detection in chapter 38 and onwards. I use a mask array for asteroids, bullets, aliens and the player ship. A mask for the player's ship is an array of 64 x 64 bytes, each with a 0 or 1 value.

Now that would be a two dimension structure, except there are 24 such masks, one for each of the 24 x 15 degree rotations.

The declaration for the player ship mask is this:

```
byte plmask[24][64][64];
```

That's a three dimension array. Most of the time you'll use single or maybe two dimension arrays.

Text case in C

It's a convention that #define names are in UPPER CASE. It makes it easy to spot them.

For variables I use camel case. The first letter is always lowercase then the first letter of every other word in the variable name is upper case. Here's an example

```
int topSpeed.
```

For functions I use pascal case where the first letter of every word in the function name is upper case.

```
Void FirstCalculation()
```

That's camelCase and PascalCase. I don't like underscores in variable or function names but that's just my preference. If it works for you use them. The only thing you should really strive for is being consistent.

Comments

Much of your programming will be reading code, perhaps your own but certainly other people's. Now even if your code is beautifully laid out, good variable and function names etc., it's highly unlikely that you will be able to understand it all exactly what it does without spending a lot of time.

Adding comments in can help understanding. I see them used as glue to help understand blocks of code and how things fit together. You might have used code from another website and want to include the URL. You'll see this later with a circle drawing algorithm, I found on StackOverflow.

In a job I had, I found a peculiar bug and after I fixed it (three hours later) I left a comment in with a short explanation and the fix.

Four years, still in the same job later I came across the bug again and found my comment. It saved me another three hours work.

Comments are a good thing and might add a few milliseconds to the compile time so don't be afraid to add them.

The // is a single-line comment. Anything after to that the end of the line is ignored by the compiler. You can have lots of comments on separate lines.

```
// Like
// This
// Example
```

You can also have them on the end of a line of code.

```
UpdateAlienTimers(); //Needed for synchronising alien shooting rates
```

But C also provides a multi-line comment that starts with /* and end with */

```
/*
Like this
Example
*/
```

That way you can have a multi-line comment without // at the start of each line. It can also be a quick way to comment out many lines of code.

You will see comments throughout the game code. I've tried to put a comment before every function. Comments should be helpful, not just say what it does but maybe why. And highight things.

For instance, as part of collision detection around chapter 40, this function is used. Here's the comment before it.

```
// Adds an object to every cell it covers. For a large asteroid 280 x 280
// This can occupy between 25, 30 or 36 cells.
void AddObjectToCells(pfirstpart objectptr) {
```

In the next chapter we'll look at loops.

Chapter 13. Loop the loops

Having data in an array is fine but we need to write code to access every element in an array. E.g. work out the total of all the elements. For this we need to make our code run in a loop.

C has four ways to do loops but the last two are rarely if ever used. We'll look at all four in this and following chapters.

1. For-Loop.
2. While-Loop
3. Do While-Loop
4. Goto -Label.

For Loop

This is the most popular type of loop. I counted how many for-loops are in the final version of the asteroid game and there are 54 of them!

There are just six while-loops, three do-while loops and no Gotos. We'll start with for-loops

A for-loop looks like this with three loop sections before the body of the loop separated by semi-colons. The three loop sections are between the (). The body is the bit between { and }.

```
for (init variable; end condition; alter variable) {
   Do something code.
}
```

- **Init variable** sets the initial value of a loop variable. It can declare it as well.

- **End condition** tests the value of the loop variable to see if the loop has finished

- **Alter variable** changes the value of loop variable.

Let's take the car engine code from chapter 12 and instead of printing out one line for a car, let's print them all. Here's the snippet that replaces all the code in the main() { ... }

```
for (int index = 0; index < 10; index = index + 1) {
    printf("Car %d Engine CC = %d Top Speed = %.2f MPH\n", index, engineCC[index], topSpeed[index]);
}
```

This is what it outputs:

```
Car 0 Engine CC = 1600 Top Speed = 120.00 MPH
Car 1 Engine CC = 1800 Top Speed = 132.60 MPH
Car 2 Engine CC = 2000 Top Speed = 142.80 MPH
Car 3 Engine CC = 2400 Top Speed = 150.50 MPH
Car 4 Engine CC = 2500 Top Speed = 170.80 MPH
Car 5 Engine CC = 2800 Top Speed = 173.20 MPH
Car 6 Engine CC = 3500 Top Speed = 175.60 MPH
Car 7 Engine CC = 4000 Top Speed = 178.40 MPH
Car 8 Engine CC = 4500 Top Speed = 181.80 MPH
Car 9 Engine CC = 5400 Top Speed = 188.70 MPH
```

The loop variable

You can declare the index variable before the loop if you wish or as I have done in the Init variable part of the for-loop. Here's it with the loop variable declared before the for-loop

```
int index;
for (index = 0; index < 10; index = index + 1) {
    printf("Car %d Engine CC = %d Top Speed = %.2f MPH\n", index, engineCC[index], topSpeed[index]);
}
```

That produces exactly the same result. I prefer the first one as its fewer lines of code.

The difference between having the variable declared before the for-loop or inside it, is that you cannot access the loop variable after the loop if you declared it inside the for-loop.

index declared before the loop

```
int index;
for (index = 0; index < 10; index = index + 1) {
printf("Car %d Engine CC = %d Top Speed = %.2f MPH\n", index, engineCC[index], topSpeed[index]);
}
int b = index;
```

That compiles ok but not the one on the next page.

Index declared inside the for-loop
```
for (int index = 0; index < 10; index = index + 1) {
printf("Car %d Engine CC = %d Top Speed = %.2f MPH\n", index,
engineCC[index], topSpeed[index]);
}
int b = index;
```

The compiler will say *identifier 'index' is undefined.*

The important thing you should take from that is the scope of the variable is for the rest of the block it is declared in.

Scope means the part of the program where the code can use that variable. You cannot access a variable until it has been declared, so scope starts with the declaration.

Here's a short program scope.c in the examples folder that won't compile because three of the variables are out of scope.

```
#include <stdio.h>
int var1=5;
int main()
{
 int var2=6;
 for (int i = 0; i < 10; i++) {
     int b = i * 2;
     int a = i + var1 + var2;
     printf("i = %d a = %d", i, a);
     int c = a * b;
     printf(" c= %d\n", c);
     int d = var3;
 }
 int var3 = var2 + c + i;
}
```

The var1 variable is declared first so it can be accessed anywhere after its declaration. Likewise var2 is declared inside main and like var1 can be accessed anywhere after that.

The loop variable i is declared in the for loop. It cannot be accessed after the for-loop so the int var3 declaration cannot access it. Also the int variable c is declared inside the body of the for-loop and cannot be accessed outside the loop.

Lastly the int d variable is declared inside the for-loop but cannot access the var3 variable because it didn't exist when d was declared. .

The int a is declared inside the for loop and can access var1, var2 and i. You'll get compile errors for all those variables that I've highlighted (d in the for loop, and both c and I in the var 3 declaration).

A shortcut way of incrementing

In the car example I used index = index + 1 to add 1 to the index variable.

You can simplify that by replacing it with index++. It means exactly the same.

You can use also ++ in expressions like this

```
int a = 6;
int b = a++;
printf("b = %d a = %d\n",b,a);
```

When you run that you'll get

b = 6 a= 7

Because the ++ is after a, it copies the value in a (6) to b then adds 1 to a.

Before or after ++?

In b=a++ the variable a is incremented after copying the value from a. You can also put the ++ before it, like this

int a = 6;
int b = ++a;
printf("b = %d a = %d\n",b,a);

You'll now get

b = 7 a= 7

It adds 1 to a then copies the value to b. So both are 7.

The good news is you can also use -- in the same way.

- With --a You'll get b = 5 a = 5. E.g. int b = --a;
- With a-- You'll get b = 6 a = 5. E.g. int b = a--;

++ and -- are the only operators you can do this with. There are other shortcuts which we'll look at later on.

Using ++ can shorten a for-loop

Instead of

for (index = 0; index < 10; index = index + 1)

We can use this

for (index = 0; index < 10; index++)

Back to the for-loop

The expressions you put in the 'init variable', 'end condition' and 'alter variable' determine if the loop ever ends and how many times you go round the loop.

The loop variable doesn't have to be an int type.

```
int i = 1;
for (char c = 'A'; c <= 'Z'; c++) {
    printf("%d : %c\n", i++, c);
}
```

That outputs

1 : A
2 : B
...
26 : Z

The loop variable can even be a float or double, but don't ever test for equality (==) with floats or doubles.

Floating point numbers aren't stored as exact values like ints. So make sure the end condition is done by a greater than or less than comparison. The expression a < b means if a is less than b then do something.

Here's how you do a for-loop with floats

```
int i = 1;
for (float v = 1.0f; v < 10.5f; v++) {
    printf("%d : %3.0f\n", i++, v);
}
```

That prints out 1 :: 1.00 and so on up to 10:: 10. Using floats or doubles as a loop variable though is not a great idea.

Empty and infinite loops

You can write an empty loop without using a loop variable e.g. for (;;). It will just loop forever which is a very bad thing.

C has a **break** statement to exit a loop. So instead of exiting because of the 'end condition' in the for-loop, it jumps out of the loop.

This code below demonstrates a **break** out of an infinite loop, looping and printing i until i reaches 13.

```
int i = 1;
for (;;) {
   printf("%d\n", i++);
   if (i == 13) break;
}
```

This last example below is a bit like questions you get in interviews. When you run this, what will it output?

First note that it adds 2 to i each time round so i goes 1,3,5 etc. It also introduces a new keyword **continue** which is the opposite of **break**. If the **continue** happens, it goes round the loop without calling printf.

```
for (int i= 1; i < 20; i +=2) {
   if (i % 3 == 0) continue;
   printf("%d\n", i);
}
```

Don't beat yourself up if you don't get it. It outputs this sequence.

1
5
7
11
13
17
19

What it does

Because of the i += 2, it only does the for-loop for odd numbers 1,3,5,7,9,11,13,15,17 and 19.

if (i % 3 ==0) means if the remainder after dividing by 3 is 0 then **continue**, i.e. skip the inside of the loop and go round the loop one more time. It does a **continue** for 3,9 and 15 so doesn't print those out.

The for-loop is a very important statement. It's not impossible to write a program without it but it would be harder and possibly more error prone.

Chapter 14. More loops

The next most popular loop after a for-loop is the while-loop. It has a very simple syntax.

```
While (expression true) {
  do something;
}
```

Here's a simple snippet that counts from 9 down to 0.

```
int i = 10;
while (i-- >0) {
   printf("%d\n", i);
}
```

Between the while and the printf, it subtracts 1 from i. So when i is 1, it does the while and prints 0 and then finishes

Of course you can do the same with a for-loop, and I much prefer it as it's easier to understand.

```
for (int i = 9; i >= 0; i--) {
    printf("%d %d\n", i, sizeof(i));
}
```

Did you spot that I had to do the test i > = 0, unlike the while which did i-- > 0. The last part of the for that alters the value of i happens after the block has been executed. So it prints 9 the first time then subtracts 1 from i.

The Bool type

I like to use while with bool variables. Other languages such as C++ and C# have this type and it takes just two values, the words true and false. Original C didn't have it but 0 was treated as false and anything non-zero as true.

while (1) is an infinite loop just like **for (;;)**.

C99 introduced bool as a type but you need to include the **stdbool** library to use it. In this example below (bool.c in the examples folder), the bool variable is set true if the value of i is greater than 20. It prints out 0,5,10,15,20 on separate lines.

```c
#include <stdio.h>
#include <stdbool.h>
int main()
{
    bool ended = false;
    int i = 0;
    while (!ended) {
        printf("%d\n", i);
        i += 5;
        ended = i > 20;
    }
    return 0;
}
```

The while (!ended) should be read as "while not ended". An exclamation mark is a not, i.e. it inverts the true/false value.

You could also spell it out explicitly with

while (ended == false)

But I think (!ended) is more natural (say it as "not ended") and slightly easier to understand.

No one forces you to use bools though I think they read easier. But any C programmer from before C99 will be at home with using an int instead, with 0 meaning false and 1 being true.

Once again this example could be done with a for-loop. This example is forbool.c.

```c
#include <stdio.h>
int main()
{
    for (int i=0;i<=20;i+=5) {
        printf("%d\n", i);
    }
    return 0;
}
```

Both output the same. I think the for-loop version is simpler but if you feel happier with the while-loop version, go with it.

The Do Loop

This inverts the logic of a while statement. The syntax is

```
do {
something
}
while (expression is true);
```

The difference between a do loop and a while loop is that the **do loop will always do the loop body at least once**. If the while expression is false **it never does the loop body at all**.

This snippet is the do loop equivalent of the while loop and prints out the same values. It's doloop.c in the examples folder.

```
bool ended = false;
int i = 0;
do {
    printf("%d\n", i);
    i += 5;
    ended = i > 20;
} while (!ended);
```

The Goto statement

C has a goto statement and it's used in conjunction with a label. It causes execution to jump i.e. carry on at the statement after the label.

A label is a name followed by a colon :. Here's an example of a goto in use.

```
    int a = 4;
    if (a == 1) goto fred;
    printf("a is not = to 1\n");
fred:
```

I've indented the label fred so it stands out. If you set a = 1 then the goto would happen and the printf would not. It's a rather bad example as you could just write it this way without a goto and it's shorter and easier to read.

```
int a = 4;
if (a != 1) {
printf("a is not = to 1\n");
}
```

Goto's got a very bad reputation in the BASIC programming language because there was no other way (other than calling a subroutine- a bit like a C function) to structure the program and programs often resembled a mass of spaghetti with Gotos all over the place.

In C you wouldn't expect to see many Gotos. I find the best use, in fact probably the only use, is for jumping out of deeply nested loops.

Nested loops

You can nest loops inside other loops, for instance a while-loop inside a for-loop, or a do-loop inside a while-loop or a for-loop inside a for-loop, in fact any combination of loop types) but if you use break to exit a loop, you only escape that loop. Goto lets you jump completely out.

Here's a made up snippet that prints out pairs of numbers.

```
for (int y = 0; y < 10; y++) {
   for (int x = 0; x < 10; x++) {
      if (x == 5 && y == 5) goto exit;
      printf("%d/%d ", y, x);
   }
   printf("\n");
}
exit:
```

The output is

0/0 0/1 0/2 0/3 0/4 0/5 0/6 0/7 0/8 0/9
1/0 1/1 1/2 1/3 1/4 1/5 1/6 1/7 1/8 1/9
2/0 2/1 2/2 2/3 2/4 2/5 2/6 2/7 2/8 2/9
3/0 3/1 3/2 3/3 3/4 3/5 3/6 3/7 3/8 3/9
4/0 4/1 4/2 4/3 4/4 4/5 4/6 4/7 4/8 4/9
5/0 5/1 5/2 5/3 5/4

If you are tempted to use a Goto be sure to have a very good reason. You should be able to write with if-else, break or continue (in loops) or functions which we'll come to before long.

Note. I used && in the example above. It means "logical and", so if (x == 5 && y == 5) means "if x equals 5 and y equals 5". There's also || which means "logical or". So if (x == 5 || y == 5) means "if x equals 5 or y equals 5".

To confuse things further there's | and & but these are "binary or" and "binary and". We'll look at these in the next chapter on operators.

That completes loops. In the next chapter we'll look at operators.

Chapter 15. About operators.

Operators are things like +, -, *, /, % and some others.

There's actually quite a few of these. For example ++,--, +=, -=, *=, /=, &=, |=, ^=,%=, << and >>.

We've already seen the [] operator for accessing the elements in arrays.

Numeric Operators

You can add with + and subtract with -

a = b + c -d;

The two character operators with an = are shortcuts. For example a += 3 is the same as a = a +3. I think the shorter version is easier to read as well. You can also use -=, *=, /= in the same way.

a /= 5 means a = a / 5.

The % operator means modulus which is like clock arithmetic. In this snippet it outputs 0,1,2,0,1,2,0,1,2,0

```
for (int i = 0; i < 10; i++)
   printf("%d\n", i % 3);
```

It's slightly confusing having % used in two different ways in the same line! Remember i % 3 means the remainder after dividing i by 3.

We'll leave the binary operators for a later chapter. These are &, |, ^, &=,|=, ^=, << and >>.

Comparison operators

We've seen the comparison operators already. These are <, >, <=, >=, ==, and !=. You probably know them all but here is a summary:

- < Less than. if (a <b) printf("a is less than b");

- \> Greater than. if (c > d) printf("a is less than b");
- \>= Greater than or equal to.
- <= Less than or equal to.
- == Equal to. if (t == k) printf("t equals k");
- != Not equal to.

The ternary operator ?:

I always think this makes your code look a little bit clever. I prefer my code to be clear, but I do like this one. In the asteroids code I've used this exactly four times.

Here's what it does. If a condition is true return one value, if it's false return another.

The syntax is

```
condition ? true-value : false-value.
char ch = 'C';
printf("Temperature is in %s\n", ch == 'F' ? "Fahrenheit" : "Celsius");
```

It does exactly the same as this below but in just one line:

```
if (ch == 'F')
    printf( "Temperature is in Fahrenheit")
else
    printf( "Temperature is in Celsius")
```

I use ?: to simplify expressions but if overused it can make your code hard to read.

Logical and Binary Ands

In the previous chapter on the Goto statement I mentioned both logical and binary ands. Both use the & and | symbols but && is a logical-and while & is a binary-and. Likewise || is a logical-or and | is a binary-or.

Logical And / Or

In a expression, say in an if statement or a while statement, you may want to check two or more conditions. Both && and || let you do that.

```
If (a==4 && b <10) {
   // Do Something
}
If (a==2 || b==9) {
   // Do Something
}
```

In the first one something happens if a equals four and b is less than ten. In the second one, a must equals 2 or b equals 9.

Those are logical ands/Ors.

Binary-and, Binary-Or and Exclusive-Or

Binary operators &,| and ^ apply to bits. Combine two chars a,b into c using these operators. The result comes from using each operator on corresponding pairs of bits.

char a = 10;
char b = 7;
char c = a & b;
printf("c = %d\n", c);

This outputs c =2. Why? We binary-and each pair of bits. If either are 0 we get 0. If both are 1 we get 1.

Operatlon	Value decimal	Binary	Decimal
	a = 10	00001010	10
	b = 7	00000111	7
Binary-And	c = a & b	00000010	2
Binary-Or	c = a | b	00001111	15
Binary-Xor	c = a ^ b	00001101	13

Now let's do this all again for Binary-or and Binary-xor, you can see those results in the table on the page before. First is Binary-or.

c = a | b;

This outputs c = 15. We binary-or each pair of bits. If either is 1 we get 1. If both are 0 we get 0.

Now there's no logical exclusive-or but there is a binary exclusive-or so once again.

c = a ^ b;

This outputs c = 13.

We exclusive-xor each pair of bits. If both are different we get 1. If both are the same we get 0.

Note I used chars here but any int type such as short int, int or long works the same way only on multiple bits.

That finishes the chapter on operators.

Chapter 16 - Structs

So far we've looked at simple variables like int a and arrays like int b[10]. In this chapter I'm going to introduce you to structs. They are called an aggregate type as they group variables together and treat them as one variable with parts that are called fields. Here's an example.

```
struct {
   float f;
   int i;
} fred;
fred.i = 7;
fred.f = 3.5f;
printf("The size of fred is %d\n", sizeof(fred));
```

This declares a struct variable called fred with a float part f and an int part i. The size it outputs is 8, made up of four bytes for the float and four for the int.

To access the fields inside a struct variable we normally use the dot notation i.e. fred.i and fred.f. When I introduce pointers, I'll show another way to access struct fields.

Type names

Char, int, float and double are names of types. We can also create a struct with a type name so you can declare instances of that struct.

The struct type name comes after the struct keyword before the {. Compare it with the struct declaration of the variable fred in the previous example.

```
struct FloatInt {
    float f;
    short i;
};
struct FloatInt fred;
fred.i = 7;
fred.f = 3.5
```

So **FloatInt** is the type name of this struct. We now declare an instance of it i.e. declaring a variable. Note that you still have to use the word struct with the type name.

Explaining struct declarations

It's quite subtle this so let me try and be really clear about it.

The first example defined and declared a struct variable called fred in one statement. It's a variable with fred after the }.

```
struct {
    float f;
    int i;
} fred;
```

The second example declared a type called a FloatInt with the name before the {. This doesn't declare a variable but a **type**.

```
struct FloatInt {
    float f;
    short i;
};
```

Once the type is declared we can now declare a variable fred of that type (FloatInt).

```
struct FloatInt fred;
fred.i = 7;
fred.f = 3.5
```

We can combine these two and both declare a type called FloatInt and an instance of it called fred in the one statement.

```
struct FloatInt {
    float f;
    short i;
} fred;
struct FloatInt fred2;
fred.i = 7;
fred.f = 3.5;
fred2 = fred;
printf("Fred2.i = %d\n", fred2.i);
```

The first struct declares the type FloatInt and a Floatint variable called fred. After the second struct declaration variable fred2 also exists. Note the line fred2 = fred. This copies both parts f and l from fred into fred2 in one statement. It copies all the fields in a struct.

I'm not keen on a declaring both a type and a variable in the one statement. I prefer to create types using structs then later declare variables of those struct types.

Structs and arrays

Declarations of structs can include arrays and you can also have arrays of structs. When you are referring to a struct type as in declaration and sizeof, you need to include the struct keyword.

```
struct FloatInts { // Declares FloatInts type
    float f;
    short i;
    int values[10];
};
struct FloatInts list[10]; // declares variable list
printf("Size of list = %d, size of FloatInts =%d\n", sizeof(list), sizeof(struct FloatInts));
```

The first struct declares a type called FloatInts. That's used in the second struct to declare an array called list holding ten FloatInts. When run this outputs:

Size of list = 480, size of FloatInts =48

Although i is a short and only two bytes in size, when it's part of a struct, the compiler aligns the individual field on four byte boundaries. Visual Studio lets you change alignments but that's a bit too advanced so I won't be covering it.

C includes an offsetof macro in the stddef.h library that lets you look at fields in a struct and how far they are relative to the start of the struct. Once again I'm referring to FloatInts so it requires struct.

This is in the file floatint.c in the examples.

```
#include <stdio.h>
#include <stddef.h>
int main()
{
    struct FloatInts {
        float f;
        short i;
        int values[10];
    };
    printf("f starts at %d\ni starts at %d\nvalues start at %d\n",
        offsetof(struct FloatInts,f),
        offsetof(struct FloatInts,i),
        offsetof(struct FloatInts,values));
    return 0;
}
```

The output is:

f starts at 0

i starts at 4

values start at 8

C lets you create data structures as complex as you wish and there's just one more to cover, pointers. But before we do those, as important as arrays, structs and pointers are functions and we'll look at those in the next chapter.

Note, I said that offsetof is a macro. For now just accept that **a macro is a block of text that gets substituted by the compiler** when you compile your code. We will cover macros in a future chapter.

typedefs

A typedef gives a type a new name. You use them with structs to avoid putting struct with the struct type.

The syntax is

Typedef type-declaration typename;

Here is a FloatInts struct defined with a typedef. Everything from struct to } is the type. You use FloatInts as the type to declare variables as you would with int. This is example floatint2.c.

```c
#include <stdio.h>
typedef struct {
    float f;
    short i;
    int values[10];
} FloatInts;
int main()
{
    FloatInts s; // look no struct needed!
    FloatInts s2;
    s.f = 47;
    s2 = s;
    printf("s2.f = %f\n", s2.f);
    return 0;
}
```

If you remove the word typedef it won't compile until you add the word struct before both declarations of s and s2.

In the next chapter, we'll look at functions, an essential building block of any C program.

Chapter 17. Functions.

A function is a block of code that is called from one or more places. All programs have a main() function and usually more depending on the complexity. So far examples have called several functions, mostly sizeof() and printf().

You can create functions that calculate and return a value. In the Asteroids game we'll create quite a few functions. There's almost a hundred but most are only a few lines long.

As a general rule, a function should be as short as possible and only do one thing. That said, you'll see a few functions in the game that break this rule. Sometimes you need to do that.

Here's an example program poly.c to calculate a polynomial. You pass in x and it calculates y = (A*x*x) + (B* x) + C.

```
#include <stdio.h>
#define A 3
#define B 6
#define C -7
int CalculatePolynomial(int x) {
    return (A * x * x) + (B * x) + C;
}
int main()
{
    for (int x = 1; x <= 4; x++) {
        int y = CalculatePolynomial(x);
        printf("X = %d Y = %d\n", x, y);
    }
    return 0;
}
```

The three #defines let me define values for A, B and C. So it's actually compiling this.

```
int CalculatePolynomial(int x) {
   return (3 * x * x) + (6 * x) -7;
}
```

The output is

X = 1 Y = 2
X = 2 Y = 17
X = 3 Y = 38
X = 4 Y = 65

Function Layout

A function is defined by these three things:

1. The type it returns, just before the function name. The CalculatePolynomial returns an int.
2. The name of the function. That's CalculatePolynomial.
3. The input parameters. These are the values passed in brackets after the function name. It's int x here.

The body of the function does the calculation and if there is a return type defined then it must have a return with the value.

It's possible to have functions that don't return a value. In that case the return type is void.

Likewise it doesn't need to have a value passed in so void can be used there like this:

```
void InitializeGameData(void) {
  // Do something
  return;
}
```

The void input data can be empty, but you always need a return type, even if it is void.

What is a void function?

It's code to do something but doesn't return a value. Here's an example from the game that calls functions to set things up.

```
// Called when player loses a life or clears Level
void ReInitGame() {
    InitPlayer(Player.lives);
    InitThrustAngles();
    InitAsteroids();
    InitBullets();
    InitExplosions();
    InitTextSprites();
}
```

Function Declarations

In the calculate polynomial example I defined the function CalculatePolynomial before main and called it in main(). If you want to define it after main(), you need to declare it first.

Here's what that example looks like when done that way. This is example poly2.c.

```c
#include <stdio.h>
#define A 3
#define B 6
#define C -7
int CalculatePolynomial(int x); // Declaration
int main()
{
   for (int x = 1; x <= 5; x++) {
      int y = CalculatePolynomial(x);
      printf("X = %d Y = %d\n", x, y);
   }
   return 0;
}
int CalculatePolynomial(int x) { // Definition
   return (A * x * x) + (B * x) + C;
}
```

A few notes on functions.

1. If you create declarations for functions then you must define the function later on.
2. You can only pass values in, not out.
3. Functions with a variable number of input parameters are called variadic. You won't use them in the game.
4. You can return a struct from a function. Here's an example.

This is example errorparm.c

```c
#include <stdio.h>
struct ErrorParm {
   int value;
   int errorNum;
};
struct ErrorParm DoCalculation(int x, int y) {
   struct ErrorParm result;
   result.errorNum = 0;
   result.value = x + y;
   if (result.value < 0) {
      result.errorNum = 1;
   }
   return result;
}
```

```
int main()
{
    int x = -6;
    int y = 5;
    struct ErrorParm calcValue;
    calcValue = DoCalculation(x, y);
    printf("Value = %d Error = %d\n", calcValue.value, calcValue.errorNum);
    return 0;
}
```

The return value struct holds both a value and an errorNum. If the calculation result is negative the errorNum is set to 1, otherwise it's 0.

Functions are a very important part of C programming, and although I said you can't pass values out of a function, once I get onto pointers, you will be able to.

We're not finished with functions yet so there's more to learn in the next chapter.

Chapter 18. More about functions.

When you declare a variable, it occupies space in RAM according to its type. An int takes four bytes, a FloatInts struct variable occupies 48 byes and 10 sized array of FloatInts takes up 480 bytes. We've seen that already in Chapter 16 on structs.

Variables are stored in one of three areas.

1. Variables declared globally, outside functions. This is determined by the compiler so it can allocate a block of known size for all non-pointer variables.
2. Variables declared inside functions are stored in **stack memory**.
3. Variables declared dynamically (we'll come to that in pointers) are stored in a block of memory called **the heap**.

Stack memory

As well as variables declared inside a function, the stack also holds the values passed into functions and the return address.

When a function is called, the address of the code just after the function call code is pushed on the stack. When a return statement is reached in the function, the top value on the stack is popped off and the computer jumps to that address.

The thing about the stack is that it's fairly limited in size. Typically it's a few Kilobytes up to a MB in size.

Some restaurants have a plate stacker which is very similar to a stack in memory.

You add plates to the plate stacker which has a spring underneath. As you add each plate the spring is compressed so the top-most plate stays level with the top of the stacker.

The key part is that you can only get plates back in reverse order. If you add four plates, call them one, two, three and four in that order then after all four are added the top one is plate four. If you lift it off then plate three is now the top stack.

Heap Memory

This is memory that's used for dynamically allocated variables and memory accessed by pointers, neither of which I've explained yet.

All of the memory that's not used for the program, main memory or the stack is available to the heap. It could be a few GB in size. If it's Windows 32 (Visual Studio refers to x86) which most programs are then you have 2 GB of ram available.

However you can change the Visual Studio configuration to produce code for 64 bit Windows (x64) and that will provide a very large chunk of your computer's RAM.

Why not 64-bit?

The game was written for 32bit Windows. Unless you have a real need for a lot of RAM, it's easier to stick with 32 bit Windows. 64-bit code is slightly slower than 32 bit due to longer instructions and also fetching data in larger chunks.

Function parameters

When you pass values in to a function, these are called the function parameters.

In the CalculatePolynomial() example (int x) is the function parameter. Just like a variable declaration you have to declare the type and name.

```
int CalculatePolynomial(int x) {
    return (A * x * x) + (B * x) + C;
}
```

Inside the function, all references to x mean the input parameter x.

You might call this in this way.

```
int a = CalculatePolynomial(10);
```

The value 10 is copied in and so this will return (3 x 10 x 10) + (6 x 10) -7 = 353 and store that in a.

The parameter values are copied so if you have a large struct then it takes a bit longer to copy the data from the struct. With pointers you can avoid this.

You can also access variables outside a function from within that function. So long as they are declared before the function and are in scope. You couldn't access variables declared inside another function, even if it was declared before this one.

It's a good programming rule to avoid accessing global variables, but sometimes you just have to. It's either that or pass them in as parameters.

The return type
The int at the front of the function tells you that CalculatePolynominal() returns an int value to you. Functions can return any type including as we've seen void which means none.

The return statement.
If your function returns a value like the CalculatePolynomial function in poly.c then it must include a return with a value.

```
int CalculatePolynomial(int x) {
    //return (A * x * x) + (B * x) + C;
}
```

If you leave off the return, as in the commented out line above with //, the Visual C compiler will complain "'CalculatePolynominal' must return a value, but that is a warning. What will generate a compile error is the variable that stores the value.

```
int y = CalculatePolynomial(x);
printf("X = %d Y = %d\n", x, y);
```

You'll get uninitialized local variable 'y' used in the printf statement above.

So functions that aren't void, must return a value.

Return in void/non-void functions

You can use return to exit from a function before the last }.

In the function DrawPlayerShip(), I check to see if the player is active. If not this returns immediately. For instance when the player has lost a life, the game continues on to let explosion's animations run to completion.

```
// Draw player ship
void DrawPlayerShip() {
    if (!Player.active) return;
… Code to draw ship
    if (!debugFlag) return;
… code to draw debug info
}
```

So during the time after the player has lost a life the DrawPlayerShip function will get called but return immediately.

Also if you haven't got the debugFlag set to 1, after drawing the ship (I've put in … to represent the code), it returns.

When the debugFlag is set, it then draws a wireframe round the ship and draws some debug information as well.

You don't need a return in a void function.

This is the code to move asteroids. No return needed.

```
// Move All Asteroids
void MoveAsteroids() {
   for (int i = 0; i<MAXASTEROIDS; i++) {
      {
         if (asteroids[i].active) {
            MoveAsteroid(i);
         }
      }
   }
}
```

You could argue that it might have been better to move this loop into MoveAsteroid and rename it to MoveAsteroids but I prefer it this way. It would have made MoveAsteroid more complicated, with everything inside the for-loop.

In the next chapter, we'll take a look at pointers.

Chapter 19. Pointers

Normally when you declare variables, there's code generated by the compiler so that when the program runs, memory is allocated for all the variables.

The computer's memory is split into different areas. Here's a simple diagram.

Code - A few KB or MB

Global variables - A few KB or MB

Heap - Most of the available ram (many GB in size)

Stack - Up to one MB

If you don't explicitly allocate memory with malloc() then the heap will be unused. We don't need to do that so you won't see any further discussion of malloc.

C includes a macro _ADDRESSOF() that tells you the address of a variable at runtime. This address changes on each run. Windows does this as a security feature, to make it much harder for malware to do nasty things.

Here's a small program called addressof.c showing _ADDRESSOF() in action.

```
#include <stdio.h>
#include <stdlib.h>
int a1;
int a2;
int main()
{
   printf("Address a1 = %p\nAddress a2 = %p\n", _ADDRESSOF(a1), _ADDRESSOF(a2));
   printf("Address of main() function = %p\n",main);
}
```

On my PC, on one run this output:

Address a1 = 009BA170
Address a2 = 009BA164

Address of main() function = 009B12A3

The %p format specifier prints out a 32 bit address in hexadecimal.

So let's take the address of a1 and store it in a variable. This is how you declare pointers p1 and p2. You have to declare the type of the variable that the pointer is pointing to. In this case p1 is pointing to a1 which is an int. So p1 is type int *.

The declaration type * such as char *, int * or float * is how you declare a pointer to a variable of that type.

```
int a1;
int a2;
int * p1 = _ADDRESSOF(a1);
int * p2 = _ADDRESSOF(a2);
```

P1 is a 32 bit variable and the value stored in it is the address of a1. The above value was 009BA170.

So here's a program addressof2.c that prints out the address of a1 and a2 then the addresses that p1 and p2 are pointing to and finally the addresses of p1 and p2.

```c
#include <stdio.h>
#include <stdlib.h>
int a1;
int a2;
int * p1 = _ADDRESSOF(a1);
int * p2 = _ADDRESSOF(a2);
int main()
{
    printf("Address of a1 = %p\nAddress of a2 = %p\n", _ADDRESSOF(a1), _ADDRESSOF(a2));
    printf("Address in p1 = %p\nAddress in p2 = %p\n", p1, p2);
    printf("Address of p1 = %p\nAddress of p2 = %p\n", _ADDRESSOF(p1), _ADDRESSOF(p2));
}
```

It can be quite confusing grasping the concept of pointers at first, so let's run this:

Address of a1 = 0108A170
Address of a2 = 0108A164
Address in p1 = 0108A170
Address in p2 = 0108A164
Address of p1 = 0108A000
Address of p2 = 0108A004

These have different addresses compared to the previous example. It's clear that the address stored in p1 is the same as the address of a1. Likewise for a2 and p2.

The last two lines show the addresses of p1 and p2. Let me repeat this in greater detail, because it can be confusing.

1. The variable a1 sits in memory at an address 0108A170.
2. This address (of a1) is different every time you run the program. It depends on where Windows loads the program in memory.
3. When the program runs we get the address of a1 using the _ADDRESSOF(a1) macro.
4. We use a pointer variable declared as int * p1 and we set the p1 value = address of a1.

Because p1 is pointing to a1, if you change the value of a1 then you change the value of what p1 is pointing to.

This is where the type associated with a pointer becomes important. If you told the compiler it was a float but it was really an int, it would treat the value incorrectly.

In this example below, I use a1 and p1 as before. A1 gets a value of 47 and then I print the values that p1 points to. That's *p1.

It then increment the contents of the int value that p1 points to. It does this with (*p1)++ and then prints out the value of a1 which has changed. This is addressof3.c.

```
#include <stdio.h>
#include <stdlib.h>
int a1;
int * p1 = _ADDRESSOF(a1);
int main()
{
    a1 = 47;
    printf("Value stored in *p1 = %d\n", *p1);
    (*p1)++;
    printf("Value stored in a1 = %d\n", a1);
}
```

The output is:

Value stored in *p1 = 47
Value stored in a1 = 48

Note. Be careful incrementing pointer values in case you increment the address not the contents of the address.

You must use brackets so that it increments the value not the the pointer. *p1++ alters the address in p1 so it no longer points to a1 but the location after it.

I suggest you reread this a few times till it sinks in. Once you get it, you know what pointers are about. That's very little more. We'll now look at what we can do with pointers.

Arrays and Pointers

Arrays and pointers have a special arrangement in that you can assign an array to a pointer, with no _ADDRESSOF needed. Here's a program that gets the address of an array in three different ways. All three output the same value. This is addressof4.c.

Please note, it generates a compiler warning but still runs.

```
#include <stdio.h>
#include <stdlib.h>
int array1[10];
int * p1 = array1;
int * p2 = _ADDRESSOF(array1);
int * p3 = _ADDRESSOF(array1[0]);
int main()
{
    printf("p1 = %p\np2 = %p\np3 = %p\n", p1, p2,p3);
}
```

It outputs three values all the same.

p1 = 008A75A0

p2 = 008A75A0

p3 = 008A75A0

You only need _ADDRESSOF when you are getting the address of a scalar variable like a1 in the previous example or the address of element array1[0].

Remember the 0'th element is the same as the start of an array. I think of [0] as being 0 * the size of one element. So [0] = 0 bytes from the start of an array [1] is 4 bytes (1 x the size of an int) away from the start and so on.

Don't forget that you declare a pointer with the type of the object that the pointer points to.

Here's examples of a pointer to an int and a pointer to a float.

int * ptrInt;
float * ptrFloat;

Now here's an array of 10 ints.

int array1[10];

Next we declare an int pointer and point it at the array.

int * pInt = array1;

If I increment the pointer variable, what does that mean?

pInt++;

It means it adds the size of the type (int = 4 bytes) to the pointer. It now points to an address four bytes further on. Let's try that with a short program. This is pointer1.c.

```
#include <stdio.h>
#include <stdlib.h>
int array1[10];
int * p1 = array1;
int main()
{
    for (int i = 0; i < 10; i++) {
        array1[i] = i * i;
    }
    for (int i = 0; i < 10; i++) {
        printf("p[%d] = %d Value of *p1 = %d\n", i, array1[i], *p1++);
    }
}
```

This fills the elements of the array1 with the square of the index. So array1[0] has the value 0, array1[1] has the value 1, array1[2] has the value 4 up to array[9] with the value 81.

The pointer variable starts pointing to array1. This is the same as pointing to array1[0]. Technically array1 is the name of the array and array1[0] is the 0th element of the array but they both refer to the same location.

The output of the program is

p[0] = 0 Value of *p1 = 0
p[1] = 1 Value of *p1 = 1
p[2] = 4 Value of *p1 = 4
p[3] = 9 Value of *p1 = 9
p[4] = 16 Value of *p1 = 16
p[5] = 25 Value of *p1 = 25
p[6] = 36 Value of *p1 = 36
p[7] = 49 Value of *p1 = 49
p[8] = 64 Value of *p1 = 64
p[9] = 81 Value of *p1 = 81

Every time we increment the pointer, it points to the next element in the array. Let's change the type of p1 to short * p1 and rerun it.

Change

int * p1 = array1;

To

short * p1 = array1;

This is the same. The type short is just a shorter version of short int.

short int * p1 = array1;

You'll get a compiler warning about incompatible types but it will compile and when you run it, you'll get.

p[0] = 0 Value of *p1 = 0
p[1] = 1 Value of *p1 = 0
p[2] = 4 Value of *p1 = 1
p[3] = 9 Value of *p1 = 0

p[4] = 16 Value of *p1 = 4
p[5] = 25 Value of *p1 = 0
p[6] = 36 Value of *p1 = 9
p[7] = 49 Value of *p1 = 0
p[8] = 64 Value of *p1 = 16
p[9] = 81 Value of *p1 = 0

That's quite bizarre. What happened?

The size of a short (i.e. a short int) is 2. So every time *p1++ was run it added two to p1 (i.e. p1 now points to an address 2 bytes further on). Let's look and see what exactly the memory looks like. We know that array1 has ten ints so it's 40 bytes long.

Viewing memory during debug in Visual Studio

In Visual Studio with this program compiled press the F10 key. It will start debugging and you'll see a small yellow arrow. Look for the for-loop with the printf and click the mouse in the gray column to the left of that for. It should be on line 12.

You should now see a red circle by the 12th line. This is a breakpoint. When the program runs it will stop here.

```
 7    int main()
 8    {
 9        for (int i = 0; i < 10; i++) {
10            array1[i] = i * i;
11        }
12        for (int i = 0; i < 10; i++) {
13            printf("p[%d] = %d Value of *p1 = %d\n", i, array1[i], *p1++);
14        }
15    }
16
```

Press the F5 key and the program runs until it hits the red spot and you'll see the yellow arrow over the red spot. If you click anywhere in the edit window (it should say pointer1.c in the tab) then move the mouse over p1 or array1, you will see a popup showing you the values.

Now we want to look at the memory bytes holding the array1 values. Click on the top menu Debug and on the popup that appears move the mouse over the first entry Windows. You'll see a second popup menu appear and near the bottom of that you'll see memory. Move the mouse over that and you'll see another popup with Memory 1, Memory 2 etc. Click Memory 1.

A new window will open and on the second line that says Address, type in p1 and press return.

You should see these numbers.

00 00 00 00 01 00 00 00 04 00 00 00 09 00 00 00 10 00 00 00 19 00 00 00
24 00 00 00 31 00 00 00 40 00 00 00 51 00 00 00 91 00 00 00

I've shown the first forty. If you take them two at a time, and group then in pairs you'll get 0000 0000 0100 0000 0400 0000 0900 0000 1000 etc.

These are 16 bit numbers in little endian order so they should be reversed. Once reversed they give 0000 0000 0001 0000 0004 0000 0009 0000 0010 which is what the output shows. 0010 is 16 in decimal.

So when you have a pointer to a type that is size n bytes (like int is 4, short is 2, char is 1), adding 1 to the pointer address actually adds n to the address.

No _ADDRESSOF?

In this example the declaration pointed p1 to the array1, that is the array of ten ints.

```
int array1[10];
short int * p1 = array1;
```

Just to confirm this, with the breakpoint in place, press F5. It will run upto the breakpoint and stop.

In the memory windows type &p1 in the address bar. You can view memory in different size chunks if you right click in the area showing the numbers in the memory window.

On mine it now shows 8 hex digit numbers starting with 003874e0. If you copy that first number (the address stored in p1) and paste it into the Address box, you can see the numbers 0,1,4,9 shown as 00000000 00000001 00000004 00000009.

If you want to set a pointer pointing at a variable, if it's an array you don't need _ADDRESSOF or &. For other variables you do.

Hiding the Memory view Window

Next time you debug, you'll see the memory view window. Just click the X at the top right to hide it. The same is true for the other debug windows.

If you close too many, just use the Debug menu item then click Windows and on the popup select the Window you want back.

Chapter 20. Text Strings

We won't be using many text strings in C so this is a fairly short overview.

Earlier I described text strings as char * type. A char is a single byte and holds a single character.

In the program below I define a c-string (reminder that's of type **char** *) called name and then call a library routine strlen() to calculate the length of name.

You'll find strlen in the string library, hence the #include <string.h>. Again remember that a #include includes the specified library. This is text1.c.

```
#include <stdio.h>
#include <stdlib.h>
#include <string.h>
char * name = "David";
int main()
{
    int len = strlen(name);
    printf("Length of string %s is %d\n", name, len);
}
```

As you'd expect this prints "Length of string David is 5".

Press F10 to start debugging then view the memory; click on the Debug menu item , then Windows, then Memory then Memory 1). Type in name at the address and press return. Right click on the memory numbers then click 1-byte integer.

The first six chars are:

44 61 76 69 64 00

At the end of this row of numbers on the right, it shows the text equivalent and this shows David with a . for the terminating 0.

> All C-Strings must have a terminating 0.

If you cursor to the 00 after the text and over type it with 64, you'll see the memory display now shows Davidd and if you step through the program. pressing F10 for each line, it will say the string now has a Length of 6.

There are a several useful string functions in the string library such as strcpy() to copy a string and strcat() to concatenate strings.

C is not a great language for text processing. For one it's awkward doing Unicode which uses characters that are 2 or 4 bytes long. It's long-winded and fiddly doing string manipulation.

This example below text2.c produces a string and printout "Score:999" and another that does "Score:1000". I use two different ways to build a string with a number.

```c
#include <stdio.h>
#include <stdlib.h>
#include <string.h>
char buffer[100];
char numberBuffer[10];
int score = 999;
int main()
{
    memcpy(buffer, "*******************", 20);
    sprintf_s(buffer, sizeof(buffer) - 1, "Score:%d", score++);
    printf("%s\n", buffer);
    _ltoa_s(score, numberBuffer,sizeof(numberBuffer)-1, 10);
    sprintf_s(buffer, sizeof(buffer) - 1, "Score:");
    strcat_s(buffer, sizeof(buffer) - 1,numberBuffer );
    printf("%s\n",buffer);
}
```

Before I explain the methods used, a bit about safe and unsafe string functions.

Safe and Unsafe C string functions

Years ago, it was found that many C functions with text handling were unsafe. If programmers didn't test their code very carefully, it was possible to have text strings longer than the memory to hold them. They would overwrite nearby variables or the stack causing exploitable bugs.

So a safe set of functions all ending in _s were created. In this example I use ltoa_s, sprintf_s and strcat_s. The sprintf_s is like printf but it 'prints' the string into an array of 100 chars called buffer.

The memcpy copies a 20 long string of * (asterisks not pointers!) into the buffer array. It's useful doing this and viewing the buffer in memory as you step through it. It's only a fill to help debugging and not needed normally.

The first sprintf_s prints "Score:" and the int value into the buffer. As sprintf_s adds a terminating zero, it's safe to print out. You never want to call printf with a C-string without a terminating 0. It will print all sorts of garbage until it finds a 0 in memory.

The code starting with _ltoa does the same but that function call converts the number into a string in a separate buffer called numberBuffer. It then concatenates that buffer on the end of buffer and prints out "Score:1000".

The _ltoa_s function does the same as a %d in the sprintf_s statement. It converts a long(l) to ascii(a) and we can use an int because long and int are both int types.

If this was _itoa instead of _ltoa then although both are int types, long values could be too big for the _itoa. So we use _ltoa.

The function strcat_s concatenates two strings and adds a terminating zero on the end . Most str functions add a terminating zero.

That's about the extent of text manipulation we'll do in the game. In the next chapter I'm going to discuss the game and that'll give us a feel for what the game has to include.

Finally after 20 chapters on C programming we are now ready to start programming the game.

What is a buffer?

I've used the term buffer several times in variable names. It's just a general name for a block of bytes.

The only difference between the unsafe and the safe _s functions is the addition of a function parameter that specifies the maximum size of the buffer in question.

By using this for that parameter in the _s functions, it means we won't accidentally overwrite memory outside the buffer area.

You'll often see code like this, either in declarations or passed as parameters into functions.

```
sizeof(buffer) - 1
```

The -1 is there because a string of say 20 characters needs 21 bytes, including the terminating 0. A buffer of 100 only allows text up to 99 characters long, so always declare one more in the buffer declaration.

If there's one thing you should never do, it's forget to leave space for the terminating 0!

Chapter 21. The Asteroids Game

Ever played the arcade game Asteroids?

A small spaceship floats around a 2D screen with asteroids floating around. To stay alive and not lose one of your three lives you must destroy all asteroids on the screen.

Then you start again on a harder level and continue until your last life is gone. How many levels can you get through?

Spaceship controls

Your spaceship fires bullets (**Space key**) and you can rotate it through a full 360 degrees either clockwise (**W key**) or anticlockwise (**Q key**). You can also accelerate in whichever direction you are facing by holding down the thrust key (**Ctrl key**) and slow down by turning 180 degrees and firing the thrust.

In the weird physics universe that arcade games inhabit, if your ship goes off one edge it comes back on the opposite. Likewise for bullets and Asteroids.

Your spaceship has an infinite amount of fuel and bullets but your spaceship's cannon stops when there are 16 bullets in play. It has to track these and has a 16 bullet limit.

As soon as a bullet hits an asteroid, or dies after a fixed period of time then more bullets can be fired but there can only be 16 onscreen at once.

When a bullet hits an asteroid, it splits into smaller asteroids. Asteroids can also bump into each other and split up.

The smallest asteroid is removed from the game screen when hit. There are four sizes of Asteroids and they are drifting in all directions and rotating slowly as well.

Special keys

You have an emergency hyperjump (**J key**) button to get you out of harm's way fast. Once used it has a three second cool-down period before it can be reused.

Also there's a shield (**S key**) that has a shield battery. While the shield is in use, the battery drains all the way from 100 towards 0. Release the key and it will slowly recharge.

The **escape key** lets you bail out of the game at any time.

In future chapters, I'll show how to install and setup the open source SDL2 library and explain how your code can use it.

You'll see how to draw graphics on screen, play sounds, read the keyboard and much more.

The basic game is under 1,000 lines of C but double that once a hi-score mode is added and level progression.

Finally we'll add some simple AI with alien saucers that periodically appears for a while seconds and shoots bullets at you.

The final version is slightly over 2,000 lines of C. Enjoy!

The Source Code

In each chapter I'll introduce new features. Some features take a few chapters; for instance the pixel perfect high speed collision detection is split across four chapters.

So along the way the game source code will be in 13 files asteroids1.c to asteroids13.c with the final full version being asteroids.c. I've zipped up each version with the name of the chapter at the end; see chapter 50 for more details.

So let's begin by creating a Solution called asteroids. Do the stuff I've taught you, remove the precompiled stuff, the three files and rename the main file to asteroids1.c. If you've forgotten how (it was 14 chapters ago!), just reread Chapter 7 Our first project.

I'll list snippets of code as we go along but I don't expect you to type in the whole thing. The 13 asteroids c files represent 13 stages along the game's development, enough so you can read the relevant source code as you read the book. I do mention the current version in the relevant chapters.

Chapter 22. Architecture of C Programs

So far we've written and compiled single file programs. But as programs become larger it often makes sense to split them into multiple files. It saves time compiling for one. If only 10% of the program changes why recompile all source code files each time even with one change?

Header and Lib files

When we need to use a function from a library, such as printf from stdio, then the program must do a #include for every library of a .h file, also known as a header file.

```
#include <stdio.h>
main( )
{
printf("hello world\n");
}
```

C includes a number of libraries with header files. But there's also an associated library file. The header file says what types and variables are provided by the library, and the library code comes in the .lib extension. This is linked into the exe that compilation produces.

You won't see .lib files for the libraries that come with the C compiler but 3rd party code such as SDL2 does provide them.

External Libraries

When we use an external library such as SDL2, it comes with a bunch of header files in one folder and a number of lib files in another.

However instead of these being all linked into one exe, they link into one or more dynamic library files with a .dll extension.

On Windows it's quite common to have an application being one exe with a number of dlls. The code in the dlls gets loaded into memory as and when it's needed, more specifically as and when a function in the library is called.

For the asteroids game, we won't be creating any dlls or lib files ourselves and the game will have just one main source code file that is compiled into one exe and use the SDL2 dlls.

Later on we will add two other source code files but don't worry about that for now.

In the next chapter we'll look at how we output graphics.

Chapter 23. Graphics

Games without graphics do exist, for instance old school text adventure games or MUDs (Multi-User Dungeons). But Asteroids without graphics wouldn't be much fun.

Neither C nor C++ has any kind of drawing capability. Back when they were first developed, computer graphics was a specialised topic. Most computers back then only output text.

But there are several libraries that can provide graphics capability and SDL2 is one of the best ones.

SDL2 Library

The SDL2 library that I've used is an open source library which means the source code is available. You won't need that unless you want to see how it works.

It has an associated SDL2_Image library as well. This is supplied with several header files, an SDL2_Image.lib file and several dll files. This is because SDL2_image supports different image types. These include jpgs, gifs, pngs and tiffs.

We'll only be using pngs and I've made all the files we'll need. We'll show some text on screen, but calling system routines to draw text with true type fonts is rarely fast enough for games.

Actually that's not strictly true; it's not unusual to use true type fonts in intro screens etc. where high speed performance is less important. True type is very flexible with fonts of any size, bold, italic etc. A bitmap font is very primitive by comparison as it's just one size. But it does print much faster.

There is a SDL2_ttf library but instead of using that I've created a bitmap font with all the letters the same width. I've written routines in C to print strings using this bitmap font.

If you wanted as an alternative, when the program starts up you could use SDL2_ttf to create the bitmaps you need, perhaps scaling the font size in proportion to the screen. But I'll leave that as an exercise for you!

When I say true type is slow, it probably takes no more than a millisecond to draw text in a specified font and size but my routine using a bitmap font will probably be a hundred times faster. We'll see how to measure execution time later.

Game Resources

I've provided the following pre-drawn graphic images. I found a free explosion generator ages ago. If you google "game maker explosion sprite" and look at images you'll find some examples.

Those images provided with the game were created by me and you can use them freely as you wish, for personal or commercial use. You download them from Github and chapter 50 explains all about that.

Here's a list of these graphics. Don't worry about doing anything with them now, we have to get you setup with SDL2 and that's in the next chapter.

This is just a list of the game's graphics requirements. Feel free to use your own, so long as they are the same size, layout and type as these.

1. a1.png-a4.png. These hold the graphic images for the asteroids in 24 rotations, so each one is rotated 15 degrees. The biggest (a1) has 24 images each 280 x 280 pixels. In a2 they are 140 x 140 pixels, a3 is 70 x 70 pixels and a4 is 35 x 35 pixels.
2. Alien.png – a 64 x 64 alien ship.
3. Bullet.png. This is 3 x 3 pixels.
4. Debug.png. This is a collection of red square wireframes starting at 280 x 280 pixels and including smaller ones. In debug mode, when the graphic is drawn, it gets a wireframe box drawn around it.

5. Explosion0.png-Explosion3.png. Each file has 64 frames each 64 x 64 pixels. It does a complete explosion animation if they are played from frame 0 to frame 63. These are arranged in 8 frames across and 8 frames down.
6. Playership.png. This has 24 images each 64 x 64 pixels of the players ship. As with Asteroids each successive frame is rotated 15 degrees clockwise.
7. Smallship.png. A single smaller version of playership that is just 24 x 32 pixels. You print three of these side by side to show three lives etc.
8. Starfield.png. A 1024 x 768 backdrop image.

In the next chapter I'll show you how to install the SDL2 library.

Chapter 24. Installing SDL2.

The SDL2 library is an open source library available from the libsdl.org website. Near the bottom left of the home page you'll see a download link. This takes you to a download page where you have several options. Make sure you click the SDL 2.0 version, not SDL 1.0.

Ignore downloading the source code. By all means download it if you want to see how it works but we won't need it.

Downloading Files from the Internet

Where those files go after downloading depends on your browser.

In Chrome if you click the three dots at the top on the right you'll see Downloads on the menu that pops up. Click it and it opens up a page that lists your downloads. Click the three dots again and it shows Open Downloads folder and clicking that opens Windows File Explorer at the downloads page.

In FireFox click the library icon; it looks like four books on a bookshelf and is on the top right. That opens a menu and one of the options is Downloads whihc has a right arrow. Click that and it takes to Show Downloads Folder. Click that and it opens Windows File Explorer.

All of the popular browsers lets you access the downloads folder and in their settings you can change the location to a folder of your own choosing.

After downloading the files, right click on each one in Windows File Explorer and in the properties look for the unblock tickbox and tick it. Windows 7 and higher automatically block files downloaded from the internet to help keep your computer safe.

Download the Runtime binaries for your type of Windows (64 bit or 32 bit). This is a zip file with a readme file and SDL2.dll. I suggest you create a SDL2 folder and under it three folders- include, dll and libs. Extract the SDL2.dll into the dll folders.

Next download the SDL2-devel-version-VC.zip in the Development Libraries section. As I write this the version is 2.0.8 so the zip file is SDL2-devel-2.0.8-VC.zip. This has folders include, docs and lib. So you can just put the contents of lib and include in the appropriate folder.

The lib folder has two sub-folders, one for 32 bit Windows and one for x64. We'll be writing for 32 bit Windows. The game won't use up that much ram and 32 bit code tends to be shorter and run faster than 64 bit.

Now we have one more library to download and setup. SDL2_image . With this you just need to download the development library, unzip and copy the libs, include files and dlls into the appropriate SDL2 folders.

There's only one SDL2_image.h file so copy that into the SDL\include folder. After copying that in, there are 86 files in total in that folder, most of them. h files.

In the SD2\lib\x66 folder you just need to copy SDL2_image.lib there. You should see SDL2.lib, SDSL2_image.lib, SDL2main.lib

135

and SDL2test.lib.

Finally in the dll folders you should copy from the SDL_image\dll folders three files: SDL2_image.dll, zlib1.dll and libpng16-16.dll to join SDL2.dll there.

32-Bit or 64-Bit?

Unless you know that your PC/laptop/desktop is 32 bit only I recommend you setup for both.

Checklist

There's a lot of instructions there and it's all too easy to miss a step, so this bit looks at what files you should have and in which folder they should be located.

I created a folder in the root of my d: drive. D:\SDL2. Feel free to use any drive. I strongly recommend you use the same folder structure as I have.

Under SDL2 there are three folders:

1. dll
2. include
3. lib

dll folder files

In the dll folder, I have the following files:

libpng16-16.dll
list.txt
SDL2.dll
SDL2_image.dll
SDL2_mixer.dll
zlib1.dll

lib folder files

In the lib folder there are two sub-folders.

1. x64
2. x86

You should have these files in both. Be very careful not to mix them up as you'll have no end of trouble. 64-bit files in x64 and 32-bit in x86.

SDL2.lib
SDL2main.lib
SDL2test.lib
SDL2_mixer.lib
SDL_mixer.lib

Include folder files

I'm not going to list them all, but there should be 85 .h files all starting with SDL_ and a couple of other files (87 in all) but we're not interested in them. Check that SDL_image.h is in there.

Setting up an empty C project

Let's create a new empty C project in Visual Studio.

Click File then New Project and a New Project Window will appear. Look down the left column for Installed and you should see Visual C++ and click on it.

On the right you should see Windows Console Application, Windows Desktop Application and the one we want Empty Project.

Where it says name, type in something like asteroids. Click browse to find somewhere to put your projects. I use D:\dev as my Windows (C:) drive is an SSD with little spare space but I have a nice big empty D: drive.

As before, in the Solution Explorer window which should now be open, select stadfx.h, targetver.h and stdafx.cpp and right click then click remove and click the Delete button.

Rename the source file from asteroids.cpp to asteroids1.c.

You do this by clicking on the file in the Solution Explorer and either click rename or press F2. Then move the cursor after the .cpp and remove the two pp by backspace. Press enter and it should show asteroids1.c.

In the main edit window remove this line in the edit Window.

#include "stdafx.h"

Feel free to edit the comments at the top as you wish.

Finally click the Project Menu option at the top of the screen and click on asteroids properties at the bottom of the menu. You should see a popup form asteroids Property Pages.

Configuring your project

Make sure the Configuration combo is set to All Configurations. Platform is Win32. Un the left side tree. Look for C/C++ then click on Precompiled Headers. Change the Precompiled Header choices from Use (.Yu) to **Not Using Precompiled Headers**. Now click the Apply button then the OK button.

Check that Visual Studio shows Debug and X86 on the toolbar. I've highlighted them.

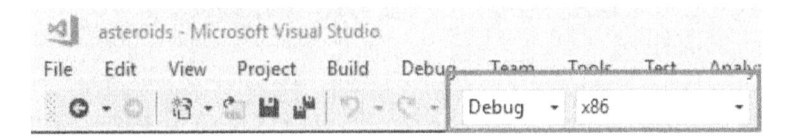

Press the F6 button and it should compile.

We now have an empty C program and are almost ready to start playing with SDL.

There's quite a bit to the Setting up SDL and it's easy to miss a step so take it one step at a time.

You'll find all the code from this book on GitHub.com and you can download it all in one big zip file. Chapter 50 has the details and I suggest you download all of them and unzip asteroids-ch25.zip ready for the next chapter.

Adding Libraries to a C or C++ project

With Visual Studio, it's the same for C and C++. A I said before there are three sets of files; the header files with a .h extension, the .lib files that hold the library code and the dlls that make up the runtime libraries.

I have all my SDL files including the SDL_Image files placed in these three folders. If you've followed my instructions and checked the checklist you should have the same folders.

- SDL\include
- SDL\lib
- SDL\dll

Let's add the include and lib paths to the project.

Open the project property pages again (from the Project menu) and on the left hand Tree click VC++ Directories. On the right you'll see General followed by seven sets of Directories.

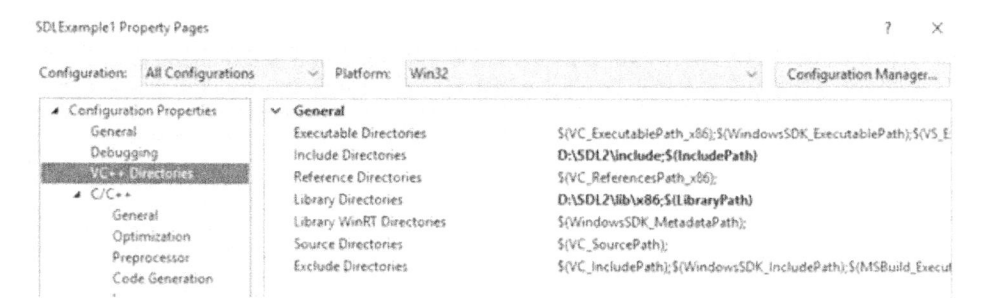

Look at the second one down, it says **Include Directories**. Click on that line on the right and you'll see a down arrow button. Click it and you'll see **<Edit...>**, which when clicked opens up an Include Directories popup. Just paste or type in your path. Mine was D:\SDL2\include. Now click OK. Now on the right of Include Directories it says

D:\SDL2\include;$(IncludePath)

Click apply then Ok.

Now select Library Directories and do the same. This time instead of the path being d:\SDL2\lib, we have to select the x86 sub-folder for Win32. So the path that I paste is D:\SDL2\lib\x86.

After pasting and clicking OK, the right hand of Library Directories says

D:\SDL2\lib\x86

Once again click Apply then Ok.

There's two more things to do.

First in the Property pages open the Linker tree item and click on input. Although we've told the compiler where the libraries are, we haven't said which ones to use. This we do by clicking on Additional Dependencies, Edit etc. and paste in these filenames.

- SDL2.lib
- SDL2main.lib
- SDL2_image.lib
- SDL2_mixer.lib

After you have edited them, the property pages should look a bit like this:

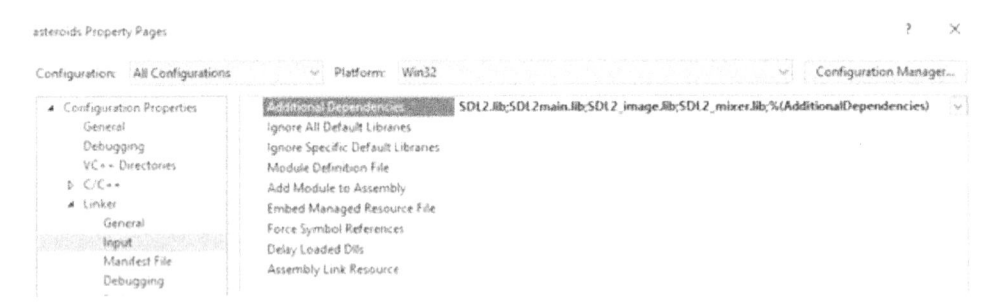

That line Additional dependencies says this:

SDL2.lib;SDL2main.lib;SDL2_image.lib;SDL2_mixer.lib;%(AdditionalDependencies)

The final step. Copy all of the dlls in the SDl2\dll folder into the Debug folder of your project.

When you compile your project with Debug and x86 settings it creates a debug folder.

After copying the dlls you should have these dlls there:

- libpng16-16.dll
- SDL2.dll
- SDL2_image.dll
- SDL2_mixer.dll
- zlib1.dll

We're now ready to roll and in the next chapter we'll compile our first SDL program.

Chapter 25. An SDL Demo program

The first SDL example is called asteroids1.c and has 133 lines of code (LOC) and throws over 1,000 random sized and random colour rectangles onto the screen. It's quite hypnotic!

Let's try running it in Visual Studio. You must have SDL2 fully installed as per my instructions in Chapter 24.

I unzipped the asteroids_ch25 file into my d: drive as d:\asteroids_ch25 and within that is a folder asteroids. If you do File Open then click Project/Solution in Visual Studio you should browse until you find asteroids_ch25 then click on that and you'll see see the asteroids folder.

Now click into that and you should see two files: asteroids.sln and asteroids.vcxproj and a Debug folder. The asteroids.sln file is the solution file and the one you should open by double clicking it. The .vcxproj file is a project within that solution.

You can have multiple projects within one solution but it's the solution you need. This should load the whole solution and project into Visual Studio. Solution Explorer should look like this on the next page.

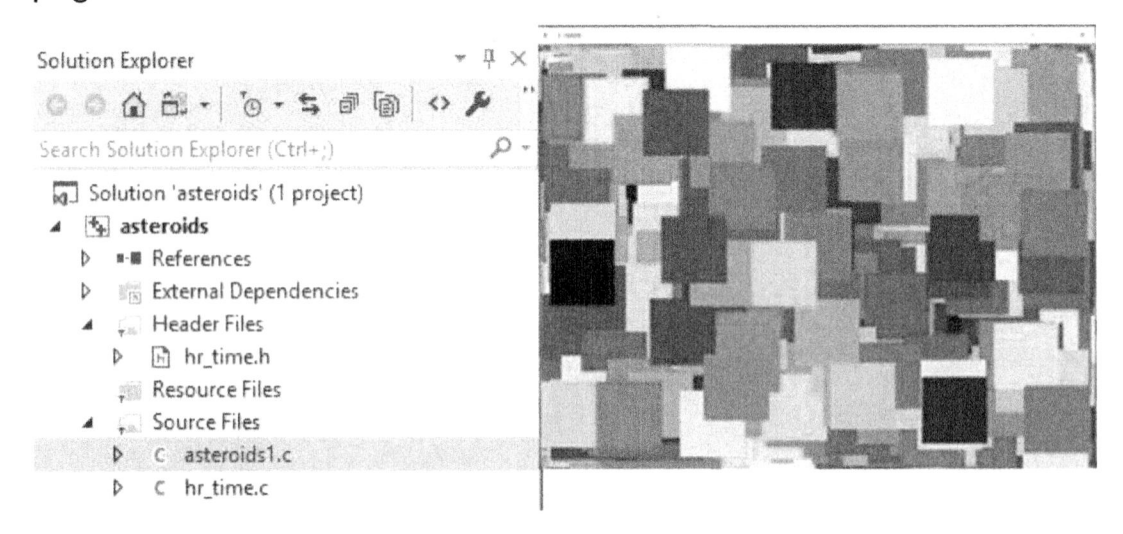

Press F6 and that will compile the asteroids1.c file. Ignore hr_time.h and .c for now we'll come to those in chapter 27.

Now press f5 to run it. You should see the rectangles above on the right.

So double-click on asteroids1.c to open it and I'll explain some of it in this chapter and the next one.

The main() at line 127 calls three functions. InitSetup() which creates a SDL window. Next is the GameLoop() and it's a feature of all computer games that they sit in a loop doing stuff until something exits the loop.

Finally FinishOff() tidies up SDL and closes the Window.

Here's InitSetup() in detail.

```
void InitSetup() {
   srand((int)time(NULL));
   SDL_Init(SDL_INIT_EVERYTHING);
   SDL_CreateWindowAndRenderer(WIDTH, HEIGHT, SDL_WINDOW_SHOWN, &screen, &renderer);
   if (!screen) {
      LogError("InitSetup failed to create window");
   }
   SetCaption("Example One");
}
```

The srand function initialises the random number generator using the time() function. This is in the time library hence the #include <time.h>. There's a Random function which calls rand (). Both srand() and rand() are in the stdlib library.

SDL_Init initialises the various SDL systems for display, keyboard, mouse and audio.

SDL_CreateWindowAndRenderer is the most important function as it creates an SDL Window of the specified width and height defined by #define values WIDTH and HEIGHT. These are #define values; remember it's a convention that #define values are always in CAPITALS.

An SDL Window is a normal Windows window that is mapped to SDL so it can display graphics at very high speed.

The &screen and &renderer are something I've not explained before. In Lines 12 and 13 I declare two pointer variables screen and renderer.

```
SDL_Window* screen = NULL;
SDL_Renderer *renderer;
```

After a call to SDL_CreateWindowAndRenderer successfully creates a window it uses these pointers to store values for variables screen and renderer. The & means address of and so the call to SDL_CreateWindowAndRenderer passes in these two addresses, the values get written back using two the pointers.

Accept for now that it works and sets these two variables. You can view the SDL documentation for this function on the SDL Wiki.

SDL_CreateWindowAndRenderer does two things - it creates a Window and a renderer in one go. Note that SDL also has these as two individual functions should you want to use them that way and later on we will.

The third parameter of the SDL_CreateWindowAndRenderer call SDL_WINDOW_SHOWN is one of a number of values depending on how you want to create the Window.

The SDL Wiki lists other flags here. There are a lot of flags listed there but for now just accept the ones I've used. Some of these other flags allow you to create an SDL Window full-screen, or without a border or as a popup menu.

After calling this, we have to check the value of screen. If it's 0 then there was a problem. Hopefully it should be non-zero.

Finally I call a function SetCaption() which sets the text on the Window frame. It just calls SDL_SetWindowTitle(screen, msg) but I find that SetCaption is easier to remember than SDL_SetWindowTitle.

That's a very quick intro so in the next chapter I'll look in more detail at the function that draws the rectangles; it's called DrawRandomRectangle and the game loop. It's just a loop in code but everything that happens in the game happens because of functions called from the game loop.

Files for this chapter

The zip file asteroids_ch25.zip contains the source files and exe plus dlls.

Remember that for now, you have to run these from within Visual Studio. Later you will be able to run them standalone.

Chapter 26. The Game Loop

Here's a listing of the Game loop function.

```c
void GameLoop() {
   int gameRunning = 1;
   while (gameRunning)
   {
      DrawRandomRectangle();
      while (SDL_PollEvent(&event)) {
         switch (event.type) {
            case SDL_KEYDOWN:
               keypressed = event.key.keysym.sym;
               if (keypressed == QUITKEY)
               {
                  gameRunning = 0;
                  break;
               }
               break;
            case SDL_QUIT: /* if mouse click to close window */
            {
               gameRunning = 0;
               break;
            }
            case SDL_KEYUP: {
               break;
            }
         } /* switch */
      } /* while SDL_PollEvent */
   }
}
```

This has two nested loops. The outer while-loop continues while gameRunning equals 1 and calls DrawRandomRectangle(). The inner while-loop calls SDL_PollEvent(). If there are no events waiting then that loop exits. The SDL_Event type lists all events.

The inner loop processes the QuitKey (i.e. the Esc key) press or the mouse click on the Windows close button.

What does DrawRandomRectangle do?

```
void DrawRandomRectangle() {
    char buff[20];
    SDL_Rect rect;
    SDL_SetRenderDrawColor(renderer, Random(256) - 1, Random(256) - 1, Random(256) - 1,255);
    rect.h = Random(100) + 20;
    rect.w = Random(100) + 20;
    rect.y = Random(HEIGHT - rect.h - 1);
    rect.x = Random(WIDTH - rect.w - 1);
    SDL_RenderFillRect(renderer,&rect);
    SDL_RenderPresent(renderer);
    rectCount++;
    if (rectCount % 1000 == 0) {
        SetCaption(SDL_Itoa(rectCount, buff, 10));
    }
}
```

This declares a 20 char buffer called buff for the SDL_Itoa call and a SDL_Rect structure with four fields w,h,x and y. These are short for width, height, x and y position.

The SDL_SetRenderDrawColor function sets the current draw colour to be purely random. Random generates a number in the range 1 to n so Random(256)-1 generates a number in the range 0 to 255.

So by calling it three times for the Red, Green and Blue components we generate one of 16 million colours.

The next four lines starting with rect.h generate a randomly sized and positioned rectangle. The y parameter is how many pixels down and the x is pixels across.

I use the convention of x being pixels across and y being pixels down a lot. Every object's coordinates are called x and y.

Flipping the screen

SDL_RenderFillRect(renderer,&rect); draws the rectangle using the renderer and the rect. However until you call SDL_RenderPresent(renderer); you'll see nothing. That's because everything is double- buffered. This avoids flicker or tearing effects.

What does that mean? Double buffered?

When you initialize a screen by calling SDL_CreateWindowAndRenderer, it decides how much video RAM (VRAM) it needs to display for the screen. It then allocates twice that amount i.e. enough for two video screens.

The video card displays one of these screens. Technically it displays the contents of one of the VRAM blocks. That's done by the hardware of the video card.

The second VRAM block is not currently being displayed and all the SDL functions that draw things always write into the VRAM block that is **not being displayed**.

Flipping What?

So we have two blocks of VRAM. The function SDL_RenderPresent flips the two memory blocks; it switches so the VRAM block that we have just being writing to is now visible. The block that was previously displayed is now no longer visible and all the SDL drawing functions now write into this.

The RenderFillRect function is very fast, on my PC it's drawing about 3,000 rectangles per second.

However the SDL_RenderPresent call is synced to the display rate so on my PC it's only doing 60 frames per second.

Faster, much faster!

Let's move the SDL_RenderPresent call into the if-block so it looks like this below.

Note that it now only executes the body of the if-block, once every ten thousand rectangles. Remember that % 10000 == 0 means if the remainder of RectCount divide by 10,000 equals 0 then do the block.

```
if (rectCount % 10000 == 0) {
    SDL_RenderPresent(renderer);
    SetCaption(SDL_ltoa(rectCount, buff, 10));
}
```

Now it's drawing about 50,000 rectangles per second! That's very fast indeed.

SDL2 uses the power of the Graphical Processor Unit to render pixels very fast indeed. It's useful to know how fast things take and we can measure time down to 1 billionth of a second (Nano seconds) and that's what we'll do in the next chapter.

Chapter 27. High Precision Timing

All processors (CPUs) for many years have included a high precision counter. This increases by one with every heartbeat of the CPU. The PC I wrote this on has a 3.5 GHZ clock. That means that every second it counts from 0 to 3,500,000,000.

By reading this counter at two points in time and dividing the difference by the CPU's frequency you get nanosecond accuracy timing.

We can time how long it takes to do things but keep in mind that Windows is running other programs simultaneously so it needs many timings to get an average.

The hr_time library

I've used a small library called hr_time which reads an internal register in the CPU. Let's modify the asteroids program and find out how long it takes to draw 100,000 rectangles.

Copy the files hr_time.h and hr_time.c into the same location as SDL_Example1.c. To add hr_time to the project right-click on Header Files then click Add then existing Item and select hr_time.h to add it to the Header Files.

Now right click on source files and add hr_time.c to that in the same way.

Next you have to modify the example source code. Add #include "hr_time.h" to the top of the asteroids1.c file. I put it under <stdlib.h>.

"SDL.h" and "hr_time.h" are in double quotes in #includes while <stdlib.h> etc are in angle brackets; this tells the C compiler where to find them.

Libraries in angle brackets are built-in libraries while the rest are added by you and must be in directories known to the project so must be inside double-quotes "".

Next we have to add a startTimer(&s); just before while (gameRunning) and then modify DrawRandomRectangle() after rectCount++ to this:

```
if (rectCount % 100000 == 0) {
   SDL_RenderPresent(renderer);
   stopTimer(&s);
   sprintf_s(buff,sizeof(buff),"%10.6f", getElapsedTime(&s));
   SetCaption(buff);
   startTimer(&s);
}
```

So after drawing 100,000 rectangles it flips the screens (remember that's what SDL_RenderPresent does) then stops the timer, calls sprintf_s (a safe version of sprintf) that calls GetElapsedTime(&s) and sets the title bar caption then it restarts the timer.

On my PC that gives a value of approximately 0.1 seconds or about a million rectangles a second.

Surprisingly, if I make the rectangles a fixed size of 120 x 120, it still takes the same time to draw them. That's rendering about 14.4 Billion pixels per second!

How does timing work?

Remember we have a CPU counter counting away at 3.5 billion times per second.

When we do startTimer(&s) we just read the counter and store the value in the stopwatch struct variable field s->start.

When we do stopTimer(&s) it again reads the counter and stores it again in the variable s->stop. This is a struct stopwatch with start and stop fields of type LARGE_INTEGER.

```
typedef struct {
    LARGE_INTEGER start;
    LARGE_INTEGER stop;
} stopWatch;
void startTimer(stopWatch *timer) {
    QueryPerformanceCounter(&timer->start);
}
double LIToSecs(LARGE_INTEGER * L) {
    LARGE_INTEGER frequency;
    QueryPerformanceFrequency(&frequency);
    return ((double)L->QuadPart / (double)frequency.QuadPart);
}
double getElapsedTime(stopWatch *timer) {
    LARGE_INTEGER time;
    time.QuadPart = timer->stop.QuadPart - timer->start.QuadPart;
    return LIToSecs(&time);
}
```

The clever bit is doing the calculation to convert it to a time. The **getElapsedTime** functions subtracts the two values in stop and start and the LIToSecs converts that into a time.

The function **QueryPerformanceCounter** reads the CPU counter and **QueryPerformanceFrequency** returns the clock frequency of the CPU.

So if the difference between the two times was 3,500 and the frequency of the CPU was 3,500,000,000 then the division would give 1/1000,000 = 1 micro-second.

In the next chapter we'll look at drawing text on the screen.

Chapter 28. Drawing Text.

Before I explain text writing, let me explain what SDL does. So far you've seen a SDL_Renderer, SDL_RenderPresent and SDL_Window. There's also SDL_Texture but I'll come to that shortly.

SDL_Window is a struct that holds all info about the Window itself: size, position, full screen, borders etc. An SDL_Renderer is a struct that holds all rendering data for a SDL_Window. It has colours and is used to render a SDL_Texture.

The reason why the rectangles drawing is so fast is that rendering is done in hardware and a SDL_Texture is a representation of pixels stored in the GPU (Graphical Processor's Unit) video memory RAM, (aka VRAM).

Let me repeat a little from chapter 26 on how the screen display is updated. There are two video memory areas, call them 1 and 2. Only one area shows on screen at a time.

This is important to remember. Anything written to a video memory area (usually by calling SDL_RenderCopy) always goes into off-screen memory. If it's displaying block 1, SDL_RenderCopy writes to block 2. If it's displaying block 2 then SDL_RenderCopy writes to block 1. It's done automatically.

This is known as double buffering. I know I mentioned this earlier but it is important. When you call SDL_RenderPresent, the display flips from showing block 1 to showing block 2 or vice versa.

So each frame, we call various functions DrawBullets(), DrawAsteroids() etc to build up the screen display etc. (We'll cover these functions later). These all call SDL_RenderCopy and it all gets written to off-screen memory. Then we call

SDL_RenderPresent and it all becomes visible at once. This happens 60 times a second.

Images

Handling picture files is not built into C but the SDL2 library has functions to do things like load images from files and copy them to the video ram (VRAM) in an SDL_Texture. Here's a smaller version of the player's ship.

I've created all the images as .png files. It's a popular graphics file format that can be output by most drawing packages. It also supports transparency. If a pixel is transparent then you see what's behind it.

Each image loads into its own Texture; i.e. picture files are copied from disk into the GPU's VRAM.

Generally it is one image per texture but you wouldn't use a whole texture for each character in a bitmap font. Instead that font has all the characters (letters, both lower and uppercase plus numbers and all the odd characters like !"£$ etc. in one image file. We use one texture for the complete font.

I've used a monospaced font (it means every character is the same width) and the first character in the font is the exclamation !. The last is lower case z. These correspond to ASCII chars 33 to 123. Here's uppercase B to L.

BCDEFGHIJKL

I've put the file text.png in a folder called images in the Visual Studio Debug folder where the exe is generated. So images/text.png is the path to the text.png file.

I'm using two textures in this example. 0 holds the backdrop image (loaded from starfield.png) and 1 the text font. The following snippet shows #defines, Textures and texturenames.

```
#define NUMTEXTURES 2
// Texture indices
#define PLBACKDROP 0
#define TEXTTEXTURE 1
SDL_Texture* textures[NUMTEXTURES];
const char * texturenames[NUMTEXTURES] = {
"images/starfield.png","images/text.png" };
```

Now that defines stuff but it doesn't load the images into the textures.

Thankfully the SDL_image library has a function **IMG_LoadTexture** to do that. To use that function we have to add the SDL_image library to our includes with #include "SDL_image.h". The **IMG_LoadTexture** creates a SDL_Texture and ties it to our renderer. I've wrapped it in a LoadTexture() function which outputs an error if it fails.

I've not said much about error handling before but if your program doesn't work as you expected, handling errors like this can save time finding out what went wrong.

This function below fails if it can't find the specified file. It calls a function called **LogError2()**. We'll come onto debugging shortly.

```
SDL_Texture* loadTexture(const char * afile, SDL_Renderer *ren) {
   SDL_Texture *texture = IMG_LoadTexture(ren, afile);
   if (texture == 0) {
      LogError2("Failed to load texture from ", afile);
   }
   return texture;
```

}

All of the textures are loaded from disk in a simple function called LoadTextures.

```
/* Loads Textures */
void LoadTextures() {
    for (int i = 0; i<NUMTEXTURES; i++) {
        textures[i] = LoadTexture(texturenames[i], renderer);
    }
}
```

It loops through the texturenames array using the NUMTEXTURES defined earlier and calls LoadTexture() for each filename. I've added a call to LoadTextures() in InitSetup().

A Bit About Compiling Visual Studio Solutions

This source file is in the source code zip file with the name **asteroids2.c**. Now something you should be aware of when you compile and run or debug exes.

By default the project file is called a solution and has .sln extension. e.g. asteroids.sln. Now all my source files are in the same folder - that's asteroids1.c, (or asteroids.c), hr_time.h, hr_time.c.

When I compile it creates a Debug or Release folder below that with the exes in. The default is Debug shown below in the white box but you can change it on the toolbar to Release. Stick to Debug.

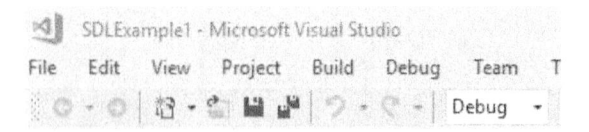

When you run or debug it, the application is run from the Debug or Release folder but *it is run as if it was launched from the project folder*. That's important and why I highlighted it.

Because of this, when the program runs in Visual Studio, it starts in the Projects folder, not the Debug folder and so the images folder is located in the project folder.

Also although this is on Windows the paths have a forward slash / not a backslash \ as is normal on Windows. This makes it compatible with Linux and Mac whose operating systems require a /.

You can use a backslash but because the backslash char in used as an 'escape' char (see below) - remember the \n at the end of strings, so you have to put it in backslash as a double backslash.

What this means, either of these two works. But it's less hassle and more portable to use the /.

```
const char * texturenames[NUMTEXTURES] = { "images/starfield.png","images/text.png" };
const char * texturenames[NUMTEXTURES] = { "images\\starfield.png","images\\text.png" };
```

What is an Escape Char?

An escape char gives a different meaning to the letter(s) following a backslash\. These are some of the escape chars that you can use in C.

'\0' - it means an actual 0 byte. Hex value 00. Often used at the end of strings.
'\n' - a newline. Same as hex value 0A.
'\r' - a carriage return. Hex value 0D.
'\t' - same as a tab char. Hex value 09.

There's a full list of escape chars on Wikipedia.

If you have the images folder in the projects folder then when you run the program it should show the backdrop. If it can't find the images files then there should be a file called errorlog.txt file in the projects folder. It will have messages like this:

Failed to load texture from images/starfield.png
Failed to load texture from images/text.png

Let's print out the numbers 1-10,000 on the screen at random locations and time how long it takes!

Printing numbers on screen

We need a TextAt() function. This prints a C-string (char *) at the specified location on screen. It uses the bitmap font file called text.png which is 1,100 x 20 pixels in size. Each character is equally spaced and 12 pixels wide by 20 high.

```
// print string text at x,y pixel coords
void TextAt(int atX, int atY, char * msg) {
    destRect.h = 23;
    destRect.w = 12;
    destRect.x = atX;
    destRect.y = atY;
    for (int i = 0; i < (int)strlen(msg); i++) {
        printch(msg[i], &destRect);
    }
}
```

How does this work?

The SDL_Rect destRect is the destination rectangle (declared globally at the start) and is set to 23 pixels high by 12. It holds an x and y which are screen positions – y is how many pixels down and x is how many across from the left edge. It also holds w and h short for width and height.

> **Here's a tip.** *Where it says SDL_Rect in the program, hold the Ctrl key and click on SDL_Rect. It should open the file SDL_rect.h and show the definition of SDL_Rect.*

It then calls printch, passing in the character and the destination rectangle.

The function printch

The function printch is a function that prints a char at the defined target rect.

```c
/* print char at rect target */
void printch(char c, SDL_Rect * target) {
    int start = (c - '!');
    if (c != ' ') {
        sourceRect.h = 23;
        sourceRect.w = 12;
        sourceRect.x = start * 12;
        sourceRect.y = 0;
        SDL_RenderCopy(renderer, textures[TEXTTEXTURE], &sourceRect, target);
    }
    (*target).x += 13;
}
```

This calculates where exactly in the text.png texture in textures[TEXTTEXTURE] the character rectangle pixels are located.

It then calls SDL_RenderCopy to render each character from the sourceRect to the target within the window. The four sourceRect. Lines assign the height and width of the character (23 and 12) then multiply the start by 12.

You'll note that we subtracted '!' from c. This is because the first character bitmap in the text.png file is for ! which is ASCII 33. C lets you use character codes like ! in maths operations.

Visual Studio lets you view and edit image files

If you use Windows File explorer to browse the images folder, you can right click on text.png and one of the popup menu options is Open in Visual Studio. After you do that, in the solution explorer it will show a list of all graphic files in that folder. You can then double click on one to show it in the main screen area like I did with test.png below.

Now click on the magnifying glass and move the mouse cursor to zoom in or out. Use the hand icon to drag the file around the screen.

Here are the first seven character bit maps in the file. Each is 12 pixels wide by 20 pixels high.

The SDL2 renderer is tied to the window so the character(s) are as always output off-screen. Here's a function that draws 500,000 random position text strings at random locations. The sprintf_s outputs the text equivalent of the variable i so 0 to 499999 becomes the text '0' to '499999'.

```
void RenderEveryThing() {
   char buffer[20];
   renderTexture(textures[PLBACKDROP], 0, 0); // Copy backdrop to off-screen memory
   startTimer(&s);
   for (int i=0;i<500000;i++) {
      int atX = Random(WIDTH-50) + 1;
      int atY = Random(HEIGHT-20) + 1;
      sprintf_s(buffer, sizeof(buffer), "%d", i);
      TextAt(atX, atY, buffer);
   }
   stopTimer(&s);
   sprintf_s(buffer, sizeof(buffer), "%10.6f", getElapsedTime(&s));
   SetCaption(buffer);
   SDL_RenderPresent(renderer); // Flip off-screen memory to be onscreen and thus visible
}
```

How It Works

Random (x) produces a random number between 0 and x-1. So Random(10) generates a number in the range 0 to 9.

The first line char buffer[20]; declares a 20 byte buffer useful for holding a text string.

The for-loop does half a million loops. This line

int atX = Random(WIDTH-50) + 1;

declares an int variable atX and sets it to a random number between 0 and WIDTH – 50 and adds 1. As WIDTH is 1024, so the actual range is 1-974.

The line after does the same for atY between 1 and 748.

Remember, SDL_RenderPresent() makes all the off-screen output visible.

This writes the backdrop then outputs about 500,000 numbers as strings in about a second. Out of curiosity, I removed the sprintf and used TextAt with

TextAt(atX, atY, SDL_Itoa(i,buffer,10));

And it does the same in 0.85 seconds. SDL_Itoa is a currently undocumented function as you can see on this page but I believe it's safe to use.

There is an Itoa function that converts a long int to ASCII in the stdlib library but SDL_ltoa seems optimised for SDL. The buffer is needed to hold the string and the function returns a pointer to it. The 10 is the base conversion i.e. decimal.

How long is a frame in time?

It's always useful to know how much processing you can do in a frame. To that end I added four int variables. You don't have to declare them on four lines, you can do them on one line like this.

```
int framecount,tickCount,lastTick, showFPS;
```

The FPS in showFPS stands for frames per second. On most laptops and desktops this tops out at 60 frames per second. However you can get much much faster frame rates. One of the options when you initialise the SDL window is to specify if it syncs to the vertical retrace.

If you don't have syncing enabled you can get frame rates of several thousand frames per second. The display isn't being refreshed at that rate, it's just the software is so fast it can redraw the screen at that rate.

We'll be syncing to the retrace so all programs will have a maximum of 60 frames per second.

The frameCount variable is incremented in RenderEverything() which now looks like this.

```
void RenderEveryThing() {
   renderTexture(textures[PLBACKDROP], 0, 0);
   startTimer(&s);
   for (int i=0;i<10000;i++) {
      int atX = Random(WIDTH-50) + 1;
      int atY = Random(HEIGHT) + 20;
      TextAt(atX, atY, SDL_ltoa(i,buffer,10));
   }
   stopTimer(&s);
   frameCount++;
   UpdateCaption();
   SDL_RenderPresent(renderer);
}
```

This new function UpdateCaption has all the logic for counting frames per second.

```
void UpdateCaption() {
   sprintf_s(buffer2, sizeof(buffer2), "%10.6f", getElapsedTime(&s));
   tickCount = SDL_GetTicks();
   if (tickCount - lastTick >= 1000) {
      lastTick = tickCount;
      if (showFPS) {
         SetCaption(buffer2);
         frameCount = 0;
      }
   }
   else if (!showFPS) {
      SetCaption(buffer2);
   }
```

}

Buffer2 (a globally declared char block) has the last frame stopwatch time written into it. The SDL_GetTicks returns a millisecond tick and is stored in tickCount. After a second has passed, tickCount will be at least 1,000 more than lastTick.

If the showFPS variable is non-zero then the SetCaption functions is called with the time as a string in buffer2.

```
/* Sets Window caption according to state - eg in debug mode or showing fps */
void SetCaption(char * msg) {
    if (showfps) {
        sprintf_s(buffer,sizeof(buffer), "Fps = %d %s", frameCount,msg);
        SDL_SetWindowTitle(screen, buffer);
    }
    else {
        SDL_SetWindowTitle(screen, msg);
    }
}
```

This either shows the time if showFPS is 0 or it prints the value in frameCount as well as the time.

For a loop value of 10,000 in RenderEveryThing, I get 80 frames per second. With 100, I get 4,500 frames per second!

Note in this version I have moved the key/mouse processing into a function that returns 0 if the escape key is pressed or the Window close button is clicked.

The GameLoop function now looks like this:

```
/* main game loop handles game play */
void GameLoop() {
    tickCount = SDL_GetTicks();
    while (ProcessEvents())
```

```
    {
        RenderEveryThing();
        //while (SDL_GetTicks() - tickCount < 17); // delay it to ~60 fps
    }
}
```

If you uncomment the while after RenderEveryThing it will waste time each loop until about 17 milliseconds have passed. This limits the frames per second to about 60.

This is a big waste of CPU processing power. If you changed the RenderEverything() loop so it ran at 1,000 fps then that means it takes one millisecond and with the time-wasting while uncommented, it would sit there doing nothing for 16 out of 17 milliseconds each frame!

Most monitors do 60 frames per second so updating faster than that is not needed. If we perform a long running operation then if it takes longer than 17 milliseconds, the display will not be smooth but in processing terms 17 milliseconds is a very long time indeed!

It's best do things in small fast operations and for asteroids, that's not really a problem.

Files for this chapter.
The zip file containing everything is asteroids_ch28.zip.

Chapter 29. More Game Elements

Conceptually there is no difference between the player's ship, an asteroid, or a bullet. All move around the screen and we display them the same way as the text was displayed.

We need to track moving elements; we need to know their speed, and rotation for the player and asteroids. So let's start coding them. This will be a long chapter as it has much of the fundamental code needed.

The player's ship.

The ship graphics are in a .png file that's 1536 pixels wide by 64 pixels high. 1536 divided by 64 = 24 so the graphic has 24 ship images each in a 64 x 64 pixel block. The first four ship images are shown below.

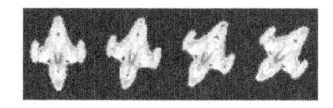

The file has 24 different rotations with the first one pointing north (0 degrees) and each successive one is 15 degrees clockwise. 15 x 24 = 360 degrees.

You could have more graphics- e.g. 36 each rotated by 10 degrees but the 24 images seem smooth enough.

I've defined a struct to hold the player ship details. I'll use structs for all the different moving objects in the game.

```
struct player {
    float x,y;
    int dir; /* 0-23 */
    float vx,vy;
    int lives;
};
```

The x and Y coordinates are floats which seems odd as pixels are integer coordinates, but moving the ship, it's best to calculate velocities in floats as well using the vx and vy fields are for. We'll display the ship with int coordinates by casting the floats to ints.

The dir field is the direction that the ship is pointing in. The lives is the number of ship lives remaining. You start with three and when they're gone, it's game over...

So we need to write functions to move the ship, render the ship on the screen and show an explosion when a life is lost. Explosions we'll leave until chapter 36.

To move the ship we need to accelerate it in whichever direction it is facing by pressing a key.

Before I start adding those functions, I need to explain a new C language feature that I'll be using.

The Switch statement

We've seen how you can use the if statement to make choices

```
if (something == 0) {
   doSomething0;
 }
 else
 if (something == 1) {
   doSomething1;
 }
```

You can add lots of ifs to handle other cases. But C (and C++) have a switch statement that makes code simpler and easier to understand.

```
switch(something) {
   case 0:
     doSomething0;
     break;
   case 1:
     doSomething1;
 doSomething2;
     break;
   case 2:
     {
       doSomething3;
       doSomething4;
       break;
     }
 }
```

This does the same as the if (something ==0) etc. You have to use the keyword **break** to end a case and curly brackets {} are optional inside a case statement. Case 1 has two statements without curly brackets while case 2 uses them.

When you see statements like doSomething, it could be a call to a function, an if statement, an assignment or any valid statement. It could also be a block of code within curly brackets.

In the program the function ProcessEvents() checks if any events such as mouse clicks or key presses have happened. It has two switch statements, one inside the other.

```
int ProcessEvents() {
while (SDL_PollEvent(&event)) {
   switch (event.type) {
      case SDL_KEYDOWN:
         keypressed = event.key.keysym.sym;
         switch (keypressed) {
            case QUITKEY:
               return 0;
            case COUNTERCLOCKWISE:
               rotateFlag = 1;
               break;
            case CLOCKWISE:
               rotateFlag = 2;
               break;
            case DEBUGKEY:
               debugFlag = 1 - debugFlag;
               showfps = 1 - showfps;
               break;
            case THRUSTKEY:
               thrustFlag = 1;
               break;
         } // switch keypressed
```

```
        case SDL_QUIT: /* if mouse click to close window */
        {
            return 0;
        }
        case SDL_KEYUP: {
            break;
        }
    } // switch event.type
} // while
return 1;
}
```

In other languages, there's a type bool but C has never had one until C99 and to get that you need #include <stdbool.h>. In this program I won't use the bool type, I like to use variables with flag as the last part of the name e.g. debugFlag to show it has two values 0 or 1.

There are a few ways to toggle a variable between 0 and 1. I use this way:

debugFlag = 1- debugFlag;

Another way is using Exclusive or. C has several binary operators such as

- **Or. a = a | b**; Combine bits. If any bit in a or in b equals 1 the result is 1.
- **And. a = a & b;** And Bits. If any bit in a or in b equals 0 the result is 0.
- **Xor. a = a ^ b;** Xor Bits. If any bit in a is different to the same bit in b the result is 1. If the two bits are the same the result is 0. Xor is pronounced exclusive-or.

A very neat way to toggle a Flag is this.

```
debugFlag ^= 1;
```

Key Handling

The outermost switch in ProcessEvents() handles the different type of events. Without getting bogged down in details, the outermost switch looks a bit like this and handles key presses down and up and clicking on the close Window X. That's the SDL_QUIT event.

```
switch (event.type) {
   case SDL_KEYDOWN:
      ...
   case SDL_QUIT: /* if mouse click to close window */
      ...
   case SDL_KEYUP: {
      ...
} // switch
```

These values SDL_QUIT etc. are defined in one of the SDL header files. Control-click on one of the SDL values to open the .h file where it's defined.

The innermost switch is for the SDL_KEYDOWN case and the code handles the different keys when pressed.

```
switch (keypressed) {
   case QUITKEY:
      ...
   case COUNTERCLOCKWISE:
      ...
   case CLOCKWISE:
      ...
   case THRUSTKEY:
      --
} // switch
```

If you leave out a break statement then it carries on to the next case below. The one exception is when the switch statement is in a function and a case has a return.

ProcessEvents requires an int value for the return. If 0 is returned then the GameLoop will exit.

When code reaches a break inside a case statement then it carries on after the switches closing bracket.

So let's look at what happens when you press the left Ctrl key. This is defined as THRUSTKEY in this #define

#define THRUSTKEY SDLK_LCTRL

Using names for the key type does makes it easier to read the program. Which is easier - THRUSTKEY or SDLK_LCTRL?

GameLoop and ProcessEvents

ProcessEvents is called every loop in the GameLoop. If you press the left control key down then it will do the while (SDL_PollEvent(&event)), followed by the switch(event.type), then case SDL_KEYDOWN.

It gets the keypressed value, does the switch(keypressed) and hits the case THRUSTKEY where it sets thrustFlag =1. It then does a break, exits the switch for keypressed at the } // switch keypressed then exits the switch for event.type and loops round to the while (SDL_PollEvent(&event)) again. Phew.

You'll notice I added comments for the switch closing brackets. It makes reading the program easier.

Ship Movements

The other two #defines rotate the player's ship; keys q and w.

#define COUNTERCLOCKWISE SDLK_q
#define CLOCKWISE SDLK_w

Now a principle of game design is when you do something that affects the ship movement, you don't move the ship directly you just change its velocity. There will be another routine in the game loop to do the movement.

So to handle the ship we need the following functions.

- RotatePlayerShip() - when CounterClockwise q or Clockwise key w pressed
- ApplyThrust () - when thrust key left ctrl pressed pressed
- MovePlayerShip - if it's got velocity it moves
- DrawPlayerShip() - draw the ship on screen.

Rotating the Ship

Let's look at RotatePlayerShip() first. The idea is simple. Press q and the ship rotates anti-clockwise or counter-clockwise. Press w and it rotates clockwise.

We need a rotateFlag to specify if the ship is rotating and if so which direction. 0 means no rotation, 1 means counter-clockwise (aka anti-clockwise) and 2 means clockwise. Sneaky here using three values in a flag variable, as normally its two.

The player's ship is 64 x 64 pixels so is rendered on-screen pretty quickly. If we change the rotation every frame it will spin too fast so we must slow it down.

So I've added a rotTimer variable. This is an int that gets its value from SDL_GetTicks() the milli-second counter. By trial and error I got a value of 40 as working well. That's 40 milliseconds each or about 25 rotations per second.

```
void RotatePlayerShip() {
    if (rotateFlag && (SDL_GetTicks() - rotTimer > 40)) {
        rotTimer = SDL_GetTicks();
        if (rotateFlag == 1) // CounterClockwise
        {
            Player.dir += 23;
```

```
            Player.dir %= 24;
      }
      else
        if (rotateFlag == 2) // Clockwise
        {
            Player.dir++;
            Player.dir %= 24;
        }
   }
}
```

What does this snippet do when the ship rotates counter-clockwise?

```
Player.dir += 23;
Player.dir %= 24;
```

The first line adds 23 to the Player.dir field. However there are only 24 rotation directions, so the second line folds it back into the range 0-23.

The % means modulus or clock arithmetic and is exactly like 24 hour clock arithmetic. If it's five O'Clock you can subtract an hour or add 23 hours, both leave it at four O'Clock.

Another way to do this would be

```
Player.dir--;
if (Player.dir < 0) {
    Player.dir += 24;
}
```

We'll see this timer comparison in the future for firing bullets etc. Now if you know any programming you'll know that timers are usually different things to how I've used them.

When I say timer here, I mean a counter that's usually holding a value read from SDL_GetTicks(). It's a SDL function that provides a number with timing accuracy to about 1/1000th of a second, i.e. a millisecond. It's more than accurate enough for timing firing periods etc.

When you lift your finger off the q or w keys, the SDL_KEYUP fires. That sets the rotateFlag to 0 and stops rotation.

Velocity in two dimensions

When you press the thrust key (the left ctrl key), the player ship accelerates in the direction it is facing. As there are 24 rotations a little math(s) is needed.

I've created two 24 x float arrays thrusty and thrusty. A function InitThrustAngles() is called once from InitGame to calculate the values in thrustx and thrusty.

It starts at 0 degrees, converts it to radians by multiplying by pi / 180 then stores the sin of the angle in thrust and the cos in thrusty. The for-loop then adds 15 degrees and so on. If you don't know trigonometry, don't worry. It works!

```
void InitThrustAngles() {
    const float pi = 3.14159265f;
    const float degreeToRad = pi / 180.0f;
    float degree = 0.0f;
    for (int i = 0; i<24; i++) {
        float radianValue = degree * degreeToRad;
        thrustx[i] = (float)sin(radianValue);
        thrusty[i] = (float)-cos(radianValue);
        degree += 15;
    }
}
```

It calls this every InitGame() is called which is a very slight waste. It would be better to calculate it once and store the values as hard coded data in the program.

The ApplyThrust function

The ApplyThrust() function is called once every 40 milliseconds and alters the x and y velocities.

```
void ApplyThrust() {
    if (thrustFlag && (SDL_GetTicks() - speedTimer > 40)) {
        speedTimer = SDL_GetTicks();
        Player.vx += (thrustx[Player.dir] / 3.0f);
        Player.vy += (thrusty[Player.dir] / 3.0f);
    }
}
```

The divide by 3.0f is a scaling factor to reduce the velocity. Change it to say 2.5 and the ship will move faster. Yes it's a magic value and I really should #define it and give it a name.

The MoveplayerShip function

This is called every game loop. No timers or counters are needed.

```
void MovePlayerShip() {
   Player.x += Player.vx;
   Player.y += Player.vy;
   if (Player.x <= -5)
      Player.x += WIDTH;
   else
      if (Player.x > WIDTH-4)
         Player.x = 0;
   if (Player.y <= -5)
      Player.y += HEIGHT;
   else
      if (Player.y > HEIGHT-4)
         Player.y = 0;
}
```

This adds the velocity for x and y (player.vx/vy) to the current locations then checks to see if the ship has gone off an edge and brings it on the opposite one. Weird video game physics!

Finally we display the spaceship with DrawPlayerShip(). This is called from the game loop, i.e. 60 times per second.

```
void DrawPlayerShip() {
    SDL_Rect spriterect, target;
    target.h = SHIPHEIGHT;
    target.w = SHIPWIDTH;
    target.x = (int)Player.x;
    target.y = (int)Player.y;
    spriterect.h = SHIPHEIGHT;
    spriterect.w = SHIPWIDTH;
    spriterect.x = Player.dir*SHIPWIDTH;
    spriterect.y = 0;
    SDL_RenderCopy(renderer, textures[TEXTUREPLAYERSHIP], &spriterect, &target);
}
```

The target SDL_Rect is easy enough to setup. The (int) casts convert Player.X and Player.Y to ints for the screen coordinates.

The spriterect x position indexes into the 1536 pixels wide ship graphic with 24 ships each 64 pixels wide. The first ship image is at x = 0. The next one (dir =1) is 64 pixels further on, the 30 degrees (dir =22) is 128 pixels and so on.

SDL_RenderCopy copies the ship image into off-screen VRAM.

To help with debugging, add the following code into DrawPlayerShip() after the SDL_renderCopy call.

```
if (!debugFlag) return;
// code after here is only run if debug !=0
target.w = 64;
target.h = 64;
spriterect.x = 280;
spriterect.y = 140;
spriterect.w = 66;
spriterect.h = 66;
SDL_RenderCopy(renderer, textures[TEXTUREDEBUG], &spriterect, &target);
sprintf_s(buff,sizeof(buff), "(%6.4f,%6.4f) Dir= %i", Player.x, Player.y, Player.dir);
TextAt((int)Player.x - 50, (int)Player.y + 66, buff);
sprintf_s(buff, sizeof(buff), "(%6.4f,%6.4f)", Player.vx, Player.vy);
TextAt((int)Player.x - 50, (int)Player.y + 90, buff);
```

Pressing the Tab key (#define DEBUGKEY SDLK_TAB) toggles both the showFPS and debugFlag. This draws a wireframe grid square from the debug.png image file, around the player's ship sprite.

It also displays the Players x, y and dir fields on one line and below it the vx and vy values.

Here you can see it's moving in direction 2 (30 degrees) with the coordinates and velocities in red.

The fps is showing 59 not 60 due to my forgetting to add 1 to the calculation! It's taking around 39 microseconds to do the game loop including moving and drawing the player ship and responding to key strokes.

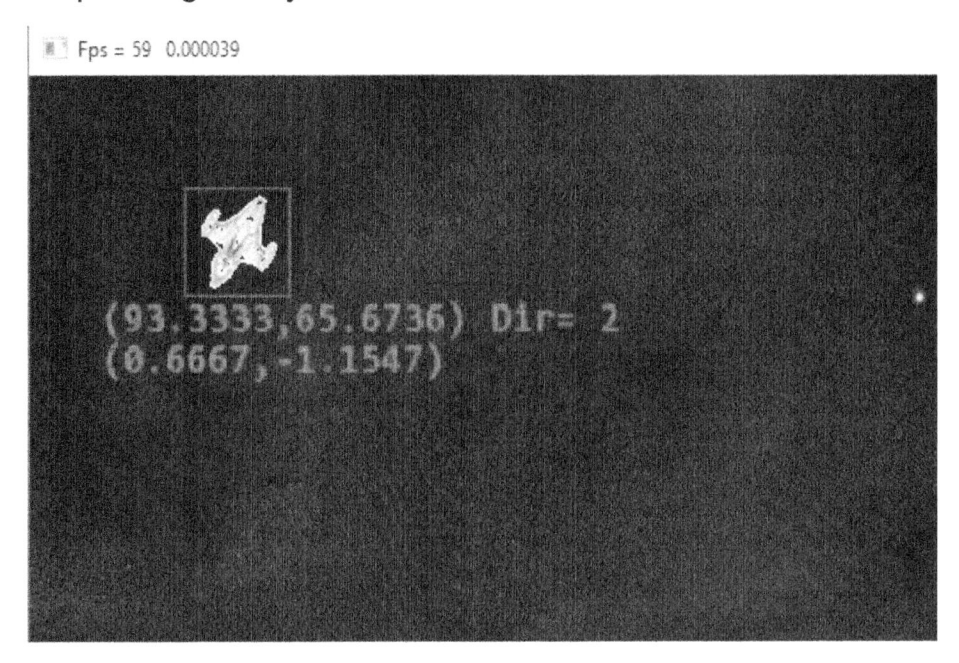

Files for this chapter.

The zip file containing everything is asteroids_ch29.zip.

Chapter 30. Adding in asteroids

Just a reminder of how much of the game has been done. It lets you move the player ship around the screen, changing direction and speeding up, or slowing down by facing backwards then hitting thrust.

Going forward we'll add the asteroids in next. The struct for an asteroid is similar to the player ship but there's additional fields needed to handle the asteroid rotation and also whether the asteroid is active. We'll use an array of structs to hold all asteroids in the game with space for 255.

```
#define MAXASTEROIDS 255
struct asteroid {
    float x,y;
    int active;
    floar xvel,yvel;
    int xtime,ytime;
    int xcount,ycount;
    int rotclockwise;
    int rottime;
    int rotcount;
    int rotdir;
    int size;
};
struct asteroid asteroids[MAXASTEROIDS];
```

As there are no asteroids on screen initially, a simple loop sets them all to inactive.

```
void InitAsteroids() {
    for (int i = 0; i<MAXASTEROIDS; i++) {
        asteroids[i].active = 0;
    }
```

}

Asteroid Graphics

Like the player's ship there are 24 rotations of each asteroid, in four sizes: 280 x 280, 140 x 140, 70 x 70 and 35 x 35, in the files a1.png, a2.png, a3.png and a4.png.

For testing the game, I added an Add Asteroid key- defined as the a key.

```
#define ADDASTEROIDKEY SDLK_a
```

Then added it as another case statement under switch(keypressed). When this key is pressed, it calls AddAsteroid(-1);

```
int FindFreeAsteroidSlot() {
    for (int i = 0; i< MAXASTEROIDS; i++) {
        if (!asteroids[i].active) {
            return i;
        }
    }
    return -1;
}
void AddAsteroid(int size) {
    int index = FindFreeAsteroidSlot();
    if (index == -1) /* table full so quietly exit */
        return;
    if (size == -1) {
        size = Random(4) - 1;
    }
    asteroids[index].active = 1;
    asteroids[index].x =(float) Random(WIDTH - size) + 20;
    asteroids[index].y = (float)Random(HEIGHT - size) + 20;
    asteroids[index].rotdir = Random(24);
```

```
    asteroids[index].rotclockwise = Random(2) - 1;
    asteroids[index].xvel = (float)4 - Random(8);
    asteroids[index].yvel = (float)4 - Random(8);
    asteroids[index].xtime = 2 + Random(5);
    asteroids[index].xcount = asteroids[index].xtime;
    asteroids[index].ytime = 2 + Random(5);
    asteroids[index].ycount = asteroids[index].ytime;
    asteroids[index].rottime = 2 + Random(8);
    asteroids[index].rotcount = asteroids[index].rottime;
    asteroids[index].size = size;
}
```

The size parameter is a value 0-3 going from largest to smallest. If -1 is passed in then it picks a size randomly. Random(n) picks a number in the range 1 to n, so for 0-3 you have to subtract 1.

FindFreeAsteroidSlo() is a function that searches for a slot for an asteroid. It returns an index 0-255 or -1 if there are no free slots because all asteroids are on screen.

You can get that by holding the a key down for a few seconds. I've modified ShowCaption() so it shows the number of active asteroids on screen. Unlike the player's ship, when they move off the screen edge, they are "killed" by setting the active to 0.

The variable numAsteroids is recalculated each time they are drawn on screen. I tested it with 256 asteroids and the frame rate stayed at 60 fps. I removed the rate capper and found that asteroids moved so fast I could never get more than ten on screen at a time. I was curious to see what frame rate it ran at with 256 asteroids on screen so I changed the case ADDASTEROIDKEY: to this.

```
case ADDASTEROIDKEY:
    for (int i = 0; i < 256; i++) {
        AddAsteroid(-1);
    }
```

With 256 asteroids on screen, it was still running at somewhere between 900 and 1,000 frames per second. It is unplayable at that speed with asteroids spinning round very rapidly and whizzing off screen so I put the rate capper back in.

Comment the line near the end that starts while (SDL_GetTicks(to see it running very fast.

This is the current GameLoop.

```
void GameLoop() {
    tickCount = SDL_GetTicks();
    while (ProcessEvents())
    {
        MoveAsteroids();
        RotatePlayerShip();
        ApplyThrust();
        MovePlayerShip();
        RenderEveryThing();
        while (SDL_GetTicks() - tickCount < 17); // frame rate cap to about 59-60 fps
    }
}
```

With a frame rate of 1,000 fps, it means all processing, moving and rendering takes about 1 millisecond. So we have tons of computing power still available.

Just for the curious, my CPU is an i7-5930K running at 3.5 Ghz. The Graphics card is an NVIDIA GeForce GTX 750 Ti and my PC is about three and a half years old.

Files for this chapter.

The zip file containing everything is asteroids_ch30.zip.

Chapter 31. Adding in bullets

We've now got the player ship rotating and moving, asteroids moving but no bullets, explosions or collisions.

In this chapter we'll add bullets which are in many ways handled like asteroids. There is a graphic but no animation or rotation. They have a time-to-live expressed as a countdown value.

When a bullet moves, its count down is decreased by one and when it hits 0 then it's removed. Plus no matter how many times you press the fire button, there can only be 16 bullets on screen at once. It's those weird arcade game physics again!

So let's add bullets. These are the usual changes.

```
#define FIREKEY SDLK_SPACE
#define MAXBULLETS 16
#define NUMTEXTURES 9
struct bullet {
    float x, y;
    int timer;
    float vx, vy;
    int ttl; // time to live
    int countdown;
};
struct bullet bullets[MAXBULLETS];
const char * texturenames[NUMTEXTURES] = {
"images/starfield.png","images/text.png","images/playership.png","images/debug.png",
"images/a1.png","images/a2.png","images/a3.png","images/a4.png","images/bullet.png" };
const int bulletx[24]={32,38,50,64,66,67,68,67,66,64,50,38,32,26,16, 0,-2,-3,-4,-3,-2,0,16,24};
const int bullety[24]={-4,-3,-2, 0,16,26,32,38,50,64,66,67,71,70,69,64 ,50,38,32,26,16,0,-2,-3};
```

```
int fireFlag, fireTimer;
```

Just as with the active field in asteroids, the ttl field in the bullet struct is used to determine if a bullet is in play or not. It's used in conjunction with countdown.

When a bullet is fired, the first thing doFireBullet() does is search the bullets array looking for an empty slot, defined as ttl equals 0. If it doesn't find one, it immediately returns.

The bulletx and bullety values are offsets to the player ship to determine where a bullet first appears. When you rotate the ship to 15, 30, 45 degrees etc, the front of the ship rotates within the 64 x 64 graphic.

So we need offsets, both horizontal and vertical to place the bullet in front of the player's ship.

We use two arrays bulletsx and bullety. There's 24 values for each, one per rotation. So when the ship is facing up in direction 0, the x offset is 32 i.e. halfway along and the y offset is -4 just 4 pixels above the nose of the ship. Also the initial velocity of the player's ship is added to the bullet speed.

If you use your own graphics with different shapes then you will have to recalculate these twenty four pairs of values.

Why countdown and ttl?

The countdown value is a timer so the bullet only moves once every three frames. Every time the bullet counter reaches 0, it is reset with the value from the timer field.

The ttl field is a timer, it determines how far the bullet travels. When the countdown reaches 0, the ttl is decremented and the countdown reset to 3.

When ttl reaches 0 the bullet is no longer moved or displayed. Of course it could hit something and vanish immediately. Collision detection is a big thing that has still to come.

If you press the Tab key to turn on debugging you'll see the ttl value for any bullets printed under the bullet.

Files for this chapter.

The zip file containing everything is asteroids_ch31.zip.

Chapter 32. A bit of C99.

One long held difference between C and C++ is where you could declare variables. The C language has had several different versions. If you come across the phrase ANSI C, it typically refers to an older version of C (aka C89) before C99.

With that older version you had to declare variables before any code. In C99, just like C++ you can declare variables in the code just before you use them.

Some programmers still prefer to declare them at the top of a function, while others including me are happy to use them as and when.

You'll often see me declare a for-loop variable like this:

```
for (int i=0;i<10;i++)
```

That variable only exists within the body of the for-loop. For instance if you look at the function initThrustAngles() where I've just added // i++.

```
// Init thrustx and thrusty[]
void InitThrustAngles() {
    const float pi = 3.14159265f;
    const float degreeToRad = pi / 180.0f;
    float degree = 0.0f;
    for (int i = 0; i<24; i++) {
        float radianValue = degree * degreeToRad;
        thrustx[i] = (float)sin(radianValue);
        thrusty[i] = (float)-cos(radianValue);
        degree += 15;
    }
    // i++
}
```

If I removed the // comment leaving i++ after the for loop's closing }, the variable i would be out of scope and the compiler would complain about an undefined identifier. To access i after the for-loop, you have to declare i before the for-loop.

I went through the program and moved variable declarations closer to where the variable is used or inside for-loops. Anything that simplifies the program is a good thing.

Comments in C

C89 (ANSI C) comments were mainly restricted to /* ... */. I say mainly because Microsoft's compiler allowed C++ single line comments that start with //. C99 now also supports those, so as most comments are single lines, I made them all //.

I also tidied the program up a bit, added comments for each of the different sets of declarations. For instance I've grouped all the #defines them by key definitions, sizes, numbers of things (Screen size et.c) and texture Indices. But there's no new files until chapter 34.

Chapter 33. Editing with Visual Studio.

Visual Studio is an IDE, that's short for Integrated Debugger and Editor. In the bad old days before IDEs you used a standalone editor to compile a program and a standalone compiler to compile it.

If there was a compile error, it would report it like this "error on line 324". You'd then have to open the editor, load the program source code, get to line 324 and fix it, save it out then exit the editor and run the compiler again. That was in the mid-1980s to 1990s or earlier.

IDEs like Visual Studio show you the error lines and make it really quick to fix the compile problems. But there are other features of Visual Studio that are useful to know and can make your life easier. Let me show you a few.

Navigate by function.

See the row above the editor but below the tabs? That row is divided into three and the third one is a pull down with a list of functions- it's showing main() below. Just select a function here and the editor will jump directly to it.

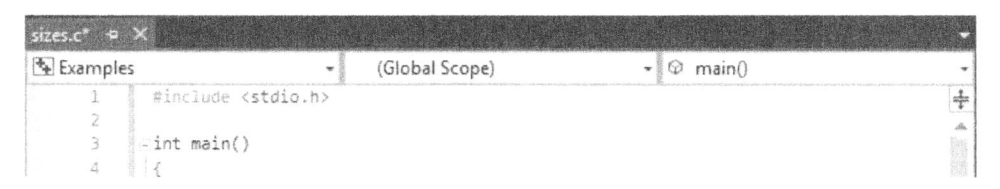

```
sizes.c*
Examples          (Global Scope)          main()
1   #include <stdio.h>
2
3   int main()
4   {
```

Bookmarks

Bookmarks are great. You can drop them anywhere in the source and click on one in a Bookmark window to quickly jump to that bookmark.

These icons on the standard toolbar are for bookmarks. Click the first one to toggle a bookmark on any line. Use the backwards and forwards arrows to move between bookmarks.

To show the bookmark window; it's on the main View menu. When you place a bookmark on a source line, it adds a line in the Bookmark Window with a name like Bookmark3. Just right click on that name and you can rename it to something meaningful.

Here's some of my bookmarks.

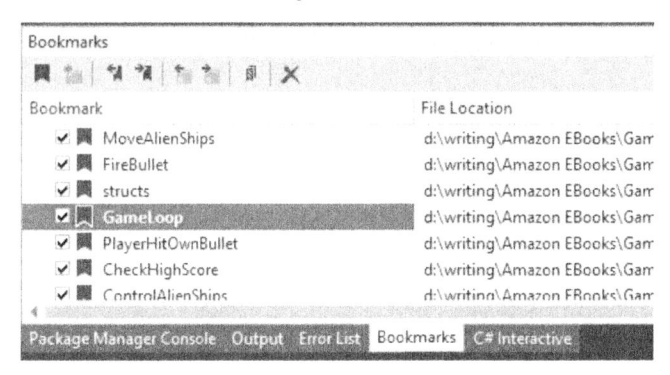

Refactoring.

When you need to change the name of a variable, const, or even a function, use the built-in refactoring.

You can search for it using Ctrl + h, but Visual Studio has you covered. Take InitPlayer. We'll rename it to InitThePlayer. Right click on InitPlayer and click Rename on the popup menu. Now type in InitThePlayer. Simples! But don't rename until after an error-free compile.

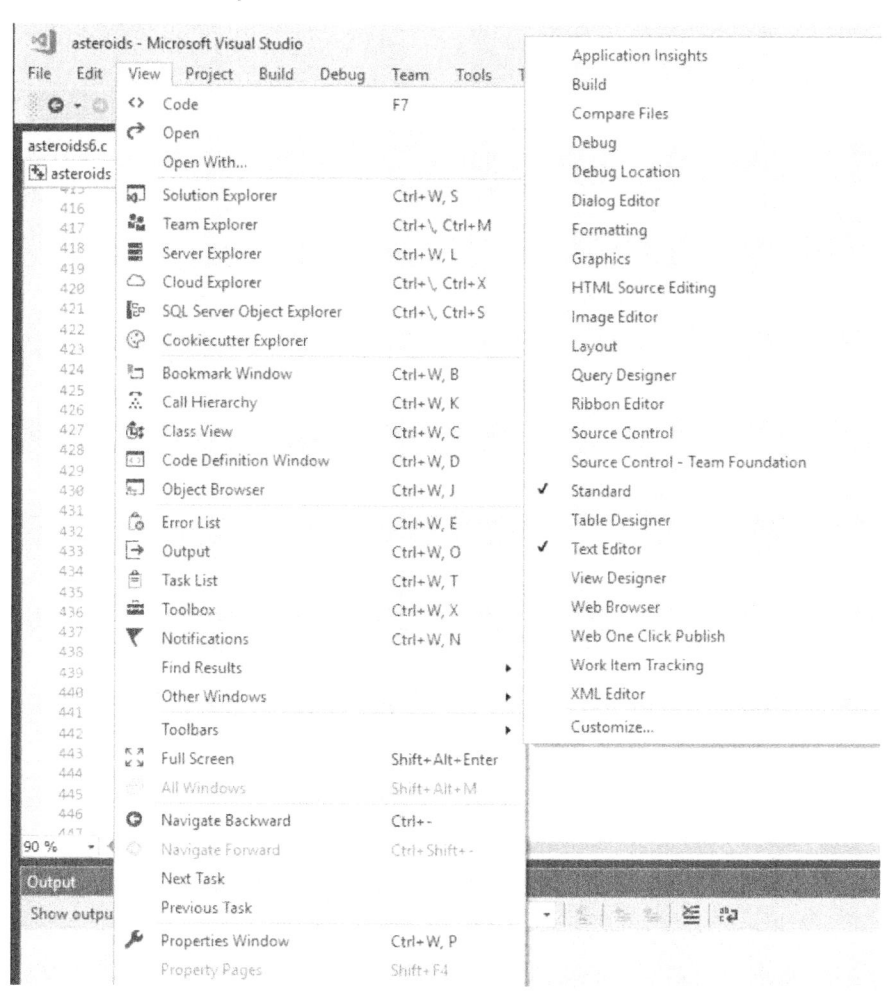

Visual Studio is probably the best IDE out there (certainly on Windows) and what you get free in the Community Edition is pretty amazing.

It's worth exploring the menus to see what else you can do. You can also enable other toolbars, about 2/3rds of the way down the View menu.

In the next chapter we'll look at restructuring C programs.

Chapter 34. Restructuring

Sooner or later you're going to need to do some restructuring. The program is currently over 600 lines long and it makes sense to put code that's finished into its own file.

Once compiled, unless you change the source file the compiler will realise that it doesn't need further compiling. This speeds up compilation of the main program.

We have to be a bit careful because anything that we need to reference from the main program has to be declared in a header file and defined in a C source code file.

Let's start in a small way by identifying those functions that can easily be moved into another file. Here are three.

- Random()
- LogError()
- LogError2()

Those are enough for now. They don't have too many dependencies.

First I'll create an empty file called lib.c and then cut/paste the function code in that file. I.e. select the text with the mouse cursor then right-click and press cut. Then in the new file, right-click and press paste.

In the Solution Explorer, right click on Source Files and then click Add then new Item. It'll popup a window showing C++ and other choices. Click on C++ Class but type in lib.c in the Name edit box near the bottom and click the Add button. An empty file called lib.c will appear in the Solution Explorer.

Open it in the editor. If it has the skeleton of a C++ class just select all (use ctrl + a) and press the Delete key. Now select the functions and cut them from asteroids6.c and paste into lib.c.

However that's just the start. Although we have the code in lib.c, we now need a header file lib.h. Click on Header Files in Solution Explorer and do the right click Add File as we did for lib.c. This time pick Header File in the Add New Item pop up form. Type in lib.h at the bottom and press add.

About Header files

Apart from the main program file, for every C code file we add , we must add a corresponding header .h file. The way the C compiler works is it reads all the files (headers, main files etc) in to memory. But if you do a #include of the same header file from several other files, the C compiler gets confused and will output compile error messages.

You've already seen other # commands such as #define and #include. I haven't explained them so now is a good time.

Before the C compiler processes source code, a program called the pre-processor reads everything in and handles words prefixed by #. **These are called pre-processor directives**. They are used to control the "architecture" of the compile, perhaps including code in a compile if a condition is true or false.

Here's some common ones.

- #define – defines a name or macro. We'll cover macros later.
- #under – the opposite of #define. It removes the name.
- #include – used to include a file in the current file.
- #warning – the compiler outputs a warning message.
- #error - the compiler stops compiling and outputs an error message.
- #if – lets you test more complicated expressions
- #ifdef name - if the name exists (which means it has been #defined previously) process the following lines until it reaches a #endif, a #elif or a #else.
- #ifndef name. Includes the following lines up to a #endif, a #elif or a #else.
- #else – defines the end of if #ifdef or #ifndef block.
- #elif – like a #else but does another #ifdef. See the examples below.
- #endif – marks the end of a conditional block.

The code after a #ifdef or #ifndef or an #else is called a conditional block.

Examples of pre-processor directives

```
#define GoodCode
#ifdef GoodCode
#include "GoodCode.h"
#else
#include "BadCode.h"
#endif
```

Because GoodCode has been defined, this will include GoodCode.h. If you remove the #define GoodCode then this will include BadCode.h.

Include Guards

So every header file that you include should have an include guard, if it's likely that other files in your project will also include the same header files.

Here's an example in hr_time.c.

```
#ifndef hr_timer
#include "hr_time.h"
#define hr_timer
#endif
```

When the C compiler reads this the first time it checks if the hr_timer has been defined with the #ifndef. On the first include it hasn't been defined so it does the #include and then creates the hr_timer name with the **#define hr_timer**. This isn't a variable, it's just a name that the C compiler tracks.

Generally for include Guard names I use the same name as the include file but without the .h extension. So for hr_time.h I did **#define hr_time**.

The lib.h file

This is what the initial lib.h looks like. These are declarations in lib.h of the functions in lib.c. Together lib.h and lib.c make up the complete library. The lib.h file tells the world (i.e. anything that includes it) what functions can be called in lib.c.

```
int Random(int max);
void LogError(char * msg);
void LogError2(const char * msg1, const char * msg2);
```

You don't have to declare every function in lib.c in the lib.h file, just those that are going to be called from somewhere else. I like to think of the functions in lib.h as public functions and the ones in lib.c that aren't in lib.h as the private functions.

Now the LogError functions need the global int variable errorCount. So that's been moved into lib.c which now looks like this. Note the #include guard at the start.

```
#ifndef lib
#include <stdio.h>
#include <stdlib.h>
#define lib
#endif
int errorCount = 0;
int Random(int max) { // returns a number between 1 and max
```

```
    return (rand() % max) + 1;
}
void LogError(char * msg) { // Log Single errors
    FILE * err;
    int error = fopen_s(&err, "errorlog.txt", "a");
    printf("%s\n", msg);
    fclose(err);
    errorCount++;
}
// Log Errors with two parameters
void LogError2(const char * msg1, const char * msg2) {
    FILE * err;
    int error = fopen_s(&err, "errorlog.txt", "a");
    fprintf_s(err, "%s %s\n", msg1, msg2);
    fclose(err);
    errorCount++;
}
```

But we have a problem now. We have to remove the errorCount from the main program (**asteroids6.c**) but we are still initialising it in initSetup() and access it from main().

What we have to do is modify the definition in the **asteroids6.c** to tell the compiler that it's an external variable.

I've added a new comment after the consts section, plus the word external in front of the declaration.

```
// external variables
extern int errorCount;
```

So the program now has five files in total. Two header files **hr_time.h** and **lib.h** and three source files **hr_time.c, lib.c** and **asteroids6.c**.

I could move the hr_timer code into the lib and that would get rid of two files but I'll leave that up to you.

Files for this chapter.

The zip file containing everything is asteroids_ch34.zip.

Chapter 35 Show the Score

We are now well on with the project. There are some major areas still to do. These include

1. Explosions.
2. Collision Detection.
3. Game Level structure.
4. Sounds.
5. Show Score and lives

My philosophy in development is to tackle the low hanging fruit first, get the simple stuff out of the way then onto the harder bits. So this chapter is about showing the score and lives on screen.

Showing Lives

I'll start by adding a new graphic. It's a smaller version of the player's ship, just 24 wide by 33 pixels tall.

As is usual with each new feature added, I've changed the version number of the file. The main program file is now **asteroids7.c**.

But first lets have a little diversion about VCS.

What is a Version Control System (VCS)?

This isn't the normal way to develop software, especially not in software houses. There's an application called a VCS (Version Control System) of which Git and Subversion are two of the best examples but there are others both open source and commercial such as Visual Source Safe, Perforce, and Mercurial.

I didn't want to add more complexity to this ebook, but if this is your first time programming then you should consider learning a VCS, and the most popular is the open source Git, created by the creator of Linux- Linus Torvalds.

The idea of a VCS is that it keeps a repository of all changes to your source code. In a team, it can be important to know who made a change and when.

So if I had been using a VCS, I'd just use Asteroids.c as the main source file all the way through. I can see what changes were made and if a bug is found, fix it.

Periodically you commit changes to the VCS. It includes tools to let you compare the current version with past ones and see what changes have happened and maybe rollback (revert) to an earlier version if you have committed something that adds a bug. Mostly though you fix the bug, or add new code and then commit it.

Adding lives etc.

When adding a new image, add it in the texturenames array and +1 to NUMTEXTURES. Then a new Texture index is added to the #defines.

In the RenderEverything() function I've added a call to DrawScoreAndLives(). Plus we need an int variable: score. There's a lives field in the Player struct set to 3 in InitPlayer().

The score is printed 30 pixels up from the bottom of the screen and the lives drawn as small ships, each 3 pixels apart, and located 70 pixels from the bottom of the screen.

```
void DrawScoreAndLives() {
   char scorebuffer[10];
   SDL_Rect destr;
   sprintf_s(scorebuffer,sizeof(scorebuffer), "%i", score);
   TextAt(25, HEIGHT-30, scorebuffer);
   destr.h = 33;
   destr.w = 24;
   destr.y = HEIGHT - 70;
   for (int i = 0; i < Player.lives; i++) {
      destr.x = (i * 30) + 50;
      SDL_RenderCopy(renderer, textures[TEXTURESMALLSHIP],NULL, &destr);
   }
}
```

The destr rect holds the screen location and size of the small player ships. The height, width and Y location are set explicitly then the x location calculated in the for-loop with values 30, 80 and 110.

The SDL_RenderCopy copies the texture for the small ship to the destr location. The NULL parameter means copy all of the source texture.

InitSetup Change

Previously I'd used the SDL_CreateWindowAndRender call to setup both screen and renderer.

However by splitting this into two calls (to SDL_CreateWindow and SDL_CreateRenderer), I was able to include the option SDL_RENDERER_PRESENTVSYNC which tells the video card to sync automatically to the display's vertical retrace.

This means it limits the frame rate to 60 FPS without me needing to do that time wasting while-loop in the GameLoop function.

This is the new InitSetup

```
void InitSetup() {
   errorCount = 0;
   srand((int)time(NULL));
   SDL_Init(SDL_INIT_EVERYTHING );
   screen= SDL_CreateWindow("Asteroids", 100, 100, WIDTH, HEIGHT, 0);
   if (!screen) {
      LogError("InitSetup failed to create window");
   }
   renderer = SDL_CreateRenderer(screen, -1, SDL_RENDERER_ACCELERATED | SDL_RENDERER_PRESENTVSYNC);
   LoadTextures();
}
```

Pause Key and Hyperspace Jump

I've added two more keys and their effects. The Pause key (the one with pause on it) pauses the game until it's pressed again. It sets pauseFlag to 1 in ProcessEvents.

In the GameLoop function I've added a CheckPause function. If the pauseFlag equals 1 then CheckPause toggles a variable called paused.

Paused is also a flag but I thought pauseFlag and pausedFlag were confusing. RenderEverything now calls DrawPauseMessage("Paused") and that function looks like this.

```
void DrawPauseMessage(char * message) {
   if (paused == 0) return;
   if (frameCount < 16 || frameCount > 45) {
      TextAt((WIDTH / 2) - 20, (HEIGHT / 2) - 20, message);
   }
```

}

The first if means this does nothing if paused equals 0. The second if looks at frameCount and only displays the message if framecount is in the range 0 - 15 or 46..60. I.E. it blinks!

The jump button (j key) sets the jumpFlag to 1. In GameLoop the CheckJump function is called which checks that the jumpFlag has been set and it's over a certain time period since jumpTimer was last updated. For jumps, it's 3 seconds which in ticks (each 1 millisecond) is 3,000.

This is CheckJump().

```
void CheckJump() {
    int hx, hy;
    if (jumpFlag && SDL_GetTicks() - jumpTimer > 3000) {
        jumpTimer = SDL_GetTicks();
        jumpFlag = 0;
        do {
            hx = 50 + Random(WIDTH - 100);
            hy = 50 + Random(HEIGHT - 100);
        }
        while(0);
        //} while (PlayerHitAsteroid(hx, hy) != -1);
        Player.x = (float)hx;
        Player.y = (float)hy;
        Player.vx = 0;
        Player.vy = 0;
    }
}
```

I've left the commented out while line (it's part of a do..while loop) in and used while(0) instead. I haven't implemented PlayerHitAsteroid() yet, so for now it's commented out.

When you are developing software, it's quite acceptable to put in calls to functions you haven't coded yet. You can either comment them out, as I did or just create the function as a stub and have it immediately return. Obviously you have to flesh it out at some point.

As we don't have collision detection yet, the do-loop only runs once.

The do loop picks random screen coordinates anywhere except in a band that's 50 high/wide at the edge. If the ship would have hit an asteroid, it tries again but that won't work until we can detect asteroids. For now, the ship will appear anywhere except near the edge.

Files for this chapter.

The zip file containing everything is asteroids_ch35.zip.

Chapter 36. Explosions

When the player's ship is hit by a bullet or an asteroid it explodes. When an asteroid hits another asteroid or is hit by a bullet, it explodes. Generally things touch- they explode.

Things you should know about game explosions; for one, the explosion doesn't move and they have a 64 frame cycle animation. There's software that generate these for example from [Sascha Williems](#) .

This uses .dds files ([Microsoft DirectDrawSurface](#)) as the base for the explosion. You can edit those with the excellent open-source [paint.net](#)

I used the Sascha Williems generator to provide the four sets of animation explosions which exports 128 x 128 sized explosions. The graphic file it exports is 1024 x 1024 pixels and arranged as 8 x 8 images.

This is the explosion struct.

```
struct explosion {
    int x, y;
    int countdown;
    int frame;
    int dimension;
};
```

In the routine DrawExplosions, spreiterect x and y fields determine where in the texture the explosion is copied from. It loads the explosion frames from the 8 x 8 image file.

Also to get the explosions centred over where the asteroid was, there's an adjustment for the 128 x 128 explosions.

```
void DrawExplosions() {
    SDL_Rect spriterect, target;
```

```
    spriterect.y = 0;
   for (int i = 0; i<MAXEXPLOSIONS; i++) {
      if (explosions[i].frame != -1) {
         int dimension = explosions[i].dimension; // 0..3
         target.x = explosions[i].x- EXPLOSIONSIZE / 2;// adjustment so explosion matches asteroid location
         target.y = explosions[i].y - EXPLOSIONSIZE / 2;
         target.h = EXPLOSIONSIZE;
         target.w = EXPLOSIONSIZE;
         spriterect.h = EXPLOSIONSIZE;
         spriterect.w = EXPLOSIONSIZE;
         int frame = explosions[i].frame;
         spriterect.y = (frame / 8) * EXPLOSIONSIZE;
         spriterect.x = (frame % 8) * EXPLOSIONSIZE;
         SDL_RenderCopy(renderer,textures[TEXTUREEXPLOSION+dimension], &spriterect, &target);
         if (debugFlag) {
            char buff[15];
             sprintf_s(buff,sizeof(buff), "X %i", explosions[i].frame);
            TextAt(target.x + 10, target.y+ EXPLOSIONSIZE, buff);
         }
      }
   }
}
```

In Sascha's generated image files (explosion0-3.png) the images are 128 x 128 pixels laid out as 8 rows of 8.

0 1 2 3 4 5 6 7
8 9 10... 15
16 ... 23
24 ... 31
...

56 57 58 59 60 61 62 63

The spriterect parameter in SDL_RenderCopy tells it the position and size of the image that we are copying from.

The spriterect .y and .x fields are the position in the image that we'll copy from. The first image is at y=0,x=0, the second one is at y=0,x=128, the third at y=0,x=256. The 8th image is on the second row, at y=128,x=0 and so on.

As we don't have collision detection yet, **I've wired up the b key (b = bang!) to blow up randomly 40%** of the asteroids on screen. It'll call this function.

```
void BlowUpAsteroids() {
   for (int i = 0; i<MAXASTEROIDS; i++) {
      if (asteroids[i].active && Random(10) <4) {
         DestroyAsteroid(i);
      }
   }
}
```

Which calls DestroyAsteroid. Now this is a longer function than usual because it has to do two things: remove the asteroid and add in smaller asteroids as it splits up.

Asteroids come in 4 sizes from 0 the biggest to 3 the smallest. When an asteroid size 0-2 is destroyed, it is split into 8 smaller asteroids. Four of these are the smallest size 3 while the other four are one size smaller than the one just destroyed. So size 0 becomes 4 x size 1 and 4 x size 3.

As the asteroid is removed, an explosion is added where the asteroid was.

```
void DestroyAsteroid(int deadIndex) {
   asteroids[deadIndex].active = 0;
   AddExplosion((int)asteroids[deadIndex].x, (int)asteroids[deadIndex].y);
   int size = asteroids[deadIndex].size;
   if (size == 3)
      return; // it's destroyed, not split so just exit
   // add in 4 smaller and 4 smallest type asteroids
   float xvel = asteroids[deadIndex].xvel;
   float yvel = asteroids[deadIndex].yvel;
   int x = (int)asteroids[deadIndex].x;
```

```
    int y = (int)asteroids[deadIndex].y;
    for (int i = 0; i<8; i++) {
        int index = FindFreeAsteroidSlot();
        if (index == -1)
            return; // no more asteroid slots free so don't add any (rare!)
        int newsize;
        if (i % 2 == 0) // if i is even add in smallest size 3
            newsize = 3;
        else
            newsize = size + 1; // next smaller size
        asteroids[index].active = 1;
        asteroids[index].x = (float)xdir[i] * sizes[size] + x;
        asteroids[index].y = (float)ydir[i] * sizes[size] + y;
        asteroids[index].rotdir = 0;
        asteroids[index].rotclockwise = Random(2) - 1;
        asteroids[index].xvel = xdir[i] * Random(4) + xvel;
        asteroids[index].yvel = ydir[i] * Random(4) + yvel;
        asteroids[index].xtime = 2 + Random(5);
        asteroids[index].xcount = asteroids[index].xtime;
        asteroids[index].ytime = 2 + Random(5);
        asteroids[index].ycount = asteroids[index].ytime;
        asteroids[index].rottime = 2 + Random(8);
        asteroids[index].rotcount = asteroids[index].rottime;
        asteroids[index].size = newsize;
    }
}
```

I've structured this so it is efficient. If the asteroid destroyed is the smallest size 3, it hits return after destroying the asteroid and adding an explosion.

Also if the asteroid added fills the asteroid table, (an unusual occurrence!) it just returns. The FindFreeAsteroidSlot() function searches for a free slot. Adding more to a full table would overflow the table and likely cause a crash.

The for-loop goes clockwise from 0 facing north, to 1 facing northeast and so on round to 7 facing northwest with A the asteroid in this 3 x 3 square.

701
6A2
543

I use the mod operator % to check for even numbers (i % 2 ==0) and those are the smallest asteroids. The others are the one size smaller asteroids that are created.

Also these 8 asteroids are given velocities in all directions but these are added to the velocity of the asteroid just destroyed.

Determining Asteroid Velocities

To determine the 8 velocities, I use two const int arrays xdir and ydir that I've added. These contain the 8 horizontal and vertical offsets around the point A in the 3 x 3 grid above.

If you look at the x,y coordinates of the point 0, the x coordinate is the same as X but the Y coordinate is 1 less. So xdir[0] equals 0 and ydir[0] equals -1. This is how the 8 values in both xdir and ydir were determined.

Show me the explosions!

Now that we can destroy asteroids, it's time to show the explosions. I've added an explosion struct, a new texture, increased NUMTEXTURES and added images/explosion.png to the list of files to load.

As with Asteroids we have an AddExplosion function at a grid coordinate x,y. This looks for a free slot where the frame value equals -1. In explosions the lowest visible frame is 0 so I chose -1 as the 'dead' value.

Now explosions don't move but we have to have a method to cycle though the frames. It's called CycleExplosions and is called from the GameLoop. Each explosion frame lasts a full frame, i.e. 1/60th of a second so a full explosion lasts 64/60 = 1.067 seconds.

And that's explosions for you. Don't forget to press the b key to see them!

Files for this chapter.
The zip file containing everything is asteroids_ch36.zip.

Chapter 37. Sounds

We need to have sounds in the game. A game without sounds would be boring though more realistic because in space there's no sound to be heard. So what sounds do we need?

1. Player ship thrust.
2. Player Ship gun firing.
3. Explosions.
4. Lose a life.

I didn't have these sound effects when I started but the internet is a wonderful resource. I searched for free sound effects and found freeSound. The v-play.net site lists 16 sites as sources for free sound effects.

I managed to find what I needed on freesound and other places but some clips were too long, so I downloaded Audacity - it's a free and open source sound editor and I used it to edit the sound effects to shorten them.

As I'm not exactly a top notch sound engineer, let's say there's room for improvement!

SDL_Mixer

A separate library, SDL_Mixer can play .wav files and other types including .mp3. For our purposes, I'm having it just play .wav.

For this you need to download the SDL2_Mixer development library for Visual Studio.

Be careful not to get SDL_Mixer, you need SDL2.Mixer although confusingly, the include file is called SDL_mixer.h. If you get the wrong SDL_Mixer, you'll know about when the program runs and asks for SDL.dll and we're using SDL2.dll. No prizes for guessing how I know this!

As before I unzipped the sdl_mixer.h into the includes folder and the lib files into lib\x86 and lib\x64 folders. Finally I copied SDL2_mixer.dll into the debug output folder where the exe is located. It's the same process as before with SDL_image and the SDL include and lib files.

If you download the runtime binaries (I used x86) and look in the folder not only will you see SDL2_mixer.dll you'll see dlls for libFLAC, libogg and others. If you are using any of these other audio formats, you need these dlls as well. I'm only playing .wav files so the SDL2_mixer.dll alone does it.

Using SDL_mixer

SDL_mixer works in this way. First you call Mix_OpenAudio to set things up and allocate memory. Next you load the four .wav files into memory. To play any of the sounds, you call Mix_PlayChannel on that sound. I've wrapped it in a function PlayASound.

The sound code

After adding #include "SDL_mixer.h" at the top, add this code at the end of InitSetup.

```
int success=Mix_OpenAudio(22050, AUDIO_S16LSB, 2, 8192);
if (success==-1 ) {
    LogError("InitSetup failed to init audio");
}
```

A value of 0 is success. You can read the documentation including function calls on SDL_mixer.

The numbers in the call to Mix_OpenAudio are 22050 = sampling frequency, AUDIO_S16LSB. This is a 16 bit signed little endian. All PCs have processors that are little-endian. The 2 is number of channels- stereo needs 2 and 8192 is the buffer size for playing the sound.

I've added the following in various places, ie. #defines near the start. I put the four wav files in the sounds folder, at the same level as the images folder. Both these folders are in the debug folder where the compiled exe is produced.

```
#define NUMSOUNDS 4
#define NUMEXPLOSIONSOUNDS 2
// sound indices
#define THRUSTSOUND 0
#define CANNONSOUND 1
#define EXPLOSIONSOUND 2
const char * soundnames[NUMSOUNDS] = {
"sounds/thrust.wav","sounds/cannon.wav","sounds/explosion1.wav","sounds/explosion2.wav" };
// Loads all sound files
void LoadSoundFiles() {
    for (int i = 0; i<NUMSOUNDS; i++) {
        sounds[i] = Mix_LoadWAV(soundnames[i]);
    }
}
void PlayASound(int soundindex) {
    int success=Mix_PlayChannel(-1, sounds[soundindex], 0);
    if (success == -1) {
        char buffer[10];
        LogError2("Mix_PlayChannel failed to play audio sound #",SDL_ltoa(soundindex,buffer,10));
    }
}
```

Plus I've added calls to PlayASound. e.g. in DoFireBullets, right after the if (index == -1) return;

```
..
if (index == -1) return; // no free slots as all bullets in play
```

```
PlayASound(CANNONSOUND);
```

And also called it for THRUSTSOUND in ApplyThrust().

```
void ApplyThrust() {
    if (thrustFlag && (SDL_GetTicks() - speedTimer > 40)) {
        speedTimer = SDL_GetTicks();
        Player.vx += (thrustx[Player.dir] / 3.0f);
        Player.vy += (thrusty[Player.dir] / 3.0f);
        PlayASound(THRUSTSOUND);
    }
}
```

And after the if (index ==-1) return in AddExplosion.

```
if (index == -1) return;
PlayASound(EXPLOSIONSOUND +
Random(NUMEXPLOSIONSOUNDS-1));
```

As there are 2 explosions sounds, the EXPLOSIONSOUND + Random(NUMEXPLOSIONSOUNDS-1) parameter is either 2 or 3. Remember Random(1) produces either 0 or 1.

In quality terms, none of the sounds are that great but they are just about good enough for this! Feel free to substitute your own.

There's now a sounds folder with the four sound files. The source code for this chapter is in asteroids9.c. When you press b to blow up the asteroids or fire the ship's cannon you'll hear the sounds.

One last addition adds extra code to the FinishOff Method. This releases memory allocated to textures and sounds and calls Mix_CloseAudio to release any other memory.

```
void DestroySounds() {
    for (int i = NUMSOUNDS - 1; i >= 0; i--) {
```

```
      Mix_FreeChunk(sounds[i]);
   }
}
void DestroyTextures() {
   for (int i = NUMTEXTURES - 1; i >= 0; i--) {
      SDL_DestroyTexture(textures[i]);
   }
}
void FinishOff() {
   DestroySounds();
   DestroyTextures();
   Mix_CloseAudio();
   SDL_DestroyRenderer(renderer);
   SDL_DestroyWindow(screen);
   SDL_Quit();
   exit(0);
}
```

And that completes sounds. The next chapter is probably the most complex in this ebook. Detecting Collisions, in fact I've split it into several chapters.

Files for this chapter.

The zip file containing everything is asteroids_ch37.zip.

Chapter 38. Detecting Collisions Part 1

You may have noticed that when you press the debug key, you get red square boxes around on-screen objects. Well not around explosions as we don't have to worry about anything hitting an explosion. This isn't Missile Command!

The red square is the bounding box for the object, it shows the square fully containing the object.

Things we do have to worry about are

- Bullets hitting an asteroid.
- Player ship hitting an asteroid.
- Asteroid hitting an asteroid.

However an addition to the game in a later chapter will be an alien saucer or 3 that occasionally shoots at the player, so bullets hitting the player ship will be the 4th condition to test for. But only alien bullets! And bullets hitting an alien saucer.

The red squares are a fast but inaccurate way of testing if collision occurs. If they overlap then there is a potential collision. But as the image below shows, they can be close enough to overlap without touching.

You'd feel peeved if your ship blew up when the red squares overlapped but the asteroid or alien bullet missed your ship.

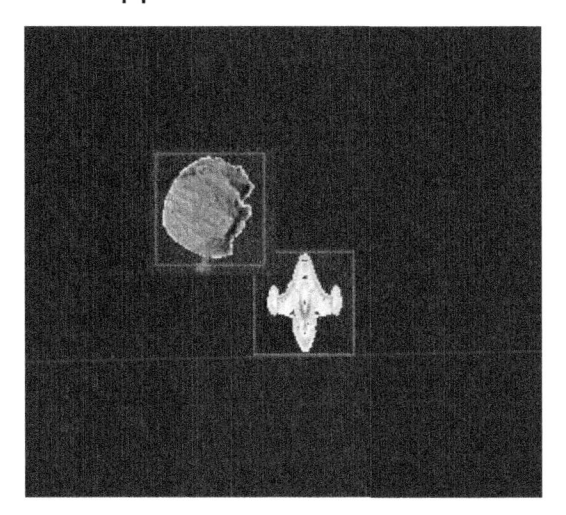

What we want is a relatively fast way to see if any non-empty pixels have overlapped. This is a method of my own making but I've probably just reinvented the wheel!

First we take the player ship graphic and create a mask from it. A mask is the same size as the graphic and if a pixel in the graphic is the background then the corresponding pixel in the mask is 0. If it has a colour then the mask pixel has a 1 value.

I wrote a program to generate masks from the 24 ship images. Each row in the player ship is 64 pixels wide so I wrote them out as 64 bytes x 64 rows and saved them out in that format into a binary file. That's 64 x 64 = 4096 bytes * 24 images, just under 100Kb. In games terms that's pretty minor.

I did the same for the Asteroids. The biggest ones are 280 x 280 pixels = 280 x 280 bytes = 78,960 bytes per image x 24 = 1,895,040 bytes. A fair bit of data but not too much.

The other asteroid sizes are smaller and total size of all these masks is around 4 Mb so it's not an onerous amount to load all masks into memory.

How do the masks work?

When two object's red boxes overlap, a potential collision has happened. We know the rotation, image type (bullet, asteroid, or players ship) and the two sets of coordinates so we can easily calculate the overlap rectangle's location and size. This is going to be a fairly small rectangle.

One thing with collision detection code is that it must be fast as with potentially tens or hundreds of objects on screen, it will be called often.

Next we do a double loop to loop through the x and y coordinates of the overlap rectangle's pixels and do an "and" (using the binary & operator) of the two corresponding bytes out of each object's masks.

If either byte is 0 then "and" will return 0. If the two anded bytes give a 1 in any position then we have a collision and immediately exit the routine.

Generating the Masks

I looked at different ways of doing this including using libpng, or writing it in C# which is somewhat easier than in C but I wanted the code to be in C and provided with this book.

I saved out the main program and stripped out everything other than the textures which I then renamed to surfaces and made SDL_Surface. Surfaces were in SDL 1 and work in main memory (RAM) rather than the GPU's VRAM.

You can create a texture from a surface but it's a bit fiddly to read pixels from textures, especially those created by IMG_LoadTexture so surfaces are easier to use.

The program genmasks.c reads in the playership, the alienship and the four asteroid files into surfaces. It then processes each surface, copying each ship or asteroid rotation into another surface imaginatively called surface.

It then reads the pixel format which is four bytes for per pixel (one for opacity and one each for red, green and blue colours) from the surface, into the variable bpp.

Then it locks the surface, and gets access to the underlying pixels with a pointer to the byte. For a non-zero byte it stores 1 in a two dimensional array data, otherwise it stores 0.

Testing the Mask generation

To test the mask generation I created a text file with one's and zero and you can see the image for the player's ship below. It looks stretched because it's a text file and the aspect ratio is incorrect but you can see the ship shape.

Also the first nine lines are shifted one byte to the left because I didn't output the row number with two digits.

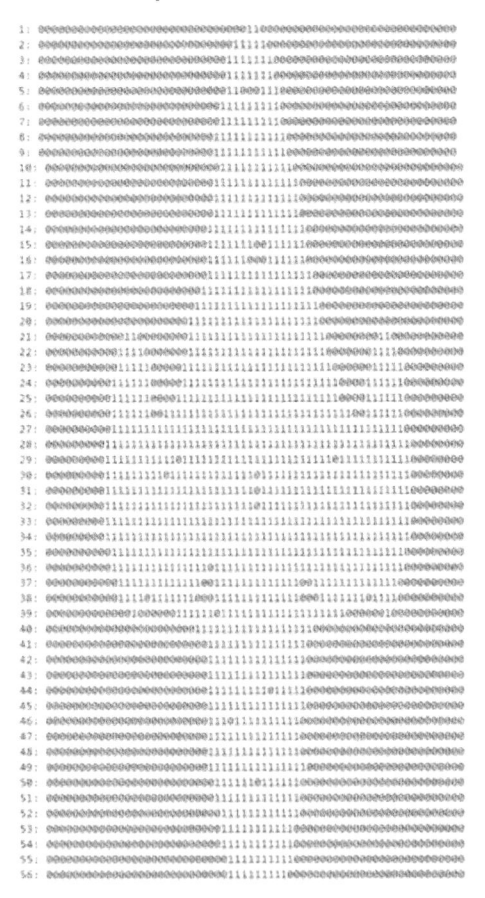

Each pixel in the mask uses one byte. This is a bit wasteful as I could have can stored 8 bits per byte.

However it means we don't have to extract the bit when comparing for a collision and that can have an impact (groan!) on processing time. The masks take up about 4 MB of ram, which is pretty small in a computer with a few GB of ram.

The alternative, using a bit to store this would have used only 1/8th of the ram, i.e. 500 bytes but it would have taken extra code to extract a bit.

This would have needed an 8 byte lookup table with the 8 bit values 128, 64,32,16,8,4,2 and 1 and the bit position (anded with 7) would give the value that you would need to extract the bit.

So it would have taken more code and a little bit longer to extract the value. It's often the case that you get a memory versus time decision and this is one where I chose memory to gain time.

To ensure it's not saving out rubbish, it creates a texture from the surface and copies it to the screen. To generate all the mask files takes under 2.5 seconds so not too bad!

The mask output

This outputs five .msk files, using fopen and "wb" parameters which write binary files; these contain any value of byte 0-255 (or hexadecimal 00-FF). There's no concept of lines in a binary file. It's just like you took a block of memory and wrote it into a file.

When you want to read or write a file in C, you call the **fopen_s** function and pass in a parameter that determines the type of file (binary or text) and whether you are reading from it or writing to it.

The ones I've used pass in two letters with r or w for read and write and b or t for binary or text file. For example "wt" writes to a text file while "rb" reads from a binary file.

```
FILE * fmask;
error = fopen_s(&fmask, textfn, "wt");
```

This returns zero if it succeeds or a non-zero error code if the file open fails; the file might be already open, in a text editor for example. The file handle is left in the first parameter, fmask in this case which is a pointer to a FILE. We use fmask to write to the file or read if you opened it for reading.

Text Files

A text file is like a binary file but usually only contains visible characters in the ASCII range 33-127 and splits the file into lines, ending in a two byte pair- values 13 and 10 on Windows. In Linux and Mac text files, lines end with just a 10 value byte.

Generally files don't play too big a part in games but you do need to know how to read and write from them.

C multi-dimensional arrays and row ordering

The great thing about binary files is that you can read them in very quickly. Just tell it how many bytes to read in and it's a single fread operation.

Now let's consider the player ship masks. We have 24 of these, each 64 x 64 bytes. The genmask program created playership.msk by writing 64 rows of 64 bytes for each of the 24 ships.

What layout should we have for our array of bytes in memory so that we can read all 24 masks into the array in a single read?

The two possible layouts are

```
byte  plmask[24[64][64];
byte  plmask[64][64][24];
```

The plmask is a three dimension array with two dimensions for each ship (64 x 64) and we have 24 of those. If we get the ordering wrong then the mask will be wrong.

So I wrote a small program to populate a 3 dimension array and see how the values are stored in it.

You can search online to find out or try experimenting. Here's the experiment listing.

```
#include <stdio.h>
int arr[2][3][4];
```

```
int * p = &arr[0][0][0];
int main() {
   int value = 1;
   for (int l = 0; l < 2; l++)
      for (int m = 0; m < 3; m++)
         for (int r = 0; r < 4; r++) {
            printf("l %i, m %i, r %i = %i\n", l, m, r, value);
            arr[l][m][r] = value++;
         }
   for (int i = 0; i < sizeof(arr)/sizeof(int); i++) {
      printf("%i : %i\n", i, *p++);
   }
   return 0;
}
```

So I declared the arr array and created a variable p that is an int pointer setting it to point to the first int in the arr structure at arr[0][0][0].

Next I populated the array with value going from 1 to 24. There are 2 x 3 x 4 = 24 elements in the array. I used l, m, and r (short for left, middle and right) to copy the value variable and add 1 to it.

Finally I printed out the 24 values in arr by using p* (value that the p pointer is pointing to) and incrementing it in the loop as confirmation that the order was 1-24.

The output from this is:

l 0, m 0, r 0 = 1
l 0, m 0, r 1 = 2
l 0, m 0, r 2 = 3
l 0, m 0, r 3 = 4
l 0, m 1, r 0 = 5

l 0, m 1, r 1 = 6
l 0, m 1, r 2 = 7
l 0, m 1, r 3 = 8
l 0, m 2, r 0 = 9
l 0, m 2, r 1 = 10
l 0, m 2, r 2 = 11
l 0, m 2, r 3 = 12
l 1, m 0, r 0 = 13
l 1, m 0, r 1 = 14
l 1, m 0, r 2 = 15
l 1, m 0, r 3 = 16
l 1, m 1, r 0 = 17
l 1, m 1, r 1 = 18
l 1, m 1, r 2 = 19
l 1, m 1, r 3 = 20
l 1, m 2, r 0 = 21
l 1, m 2, r 1 = 22
l 1, m 2, r 2 = 23
l 1, m 2, r 3 = 24
0 1
1 2
2 3
..
23 24

The lesson learned from this is that the rightmost array index changes fastest. When generating the masks the order was rotation, y then x with x changing fastest so the plmask array is also defined in that order.

`char plmask[24][64][64];` // in the order rotation,y,x

Having created a mask, I loaded it into memory with this routine and then output as a text file with '0' and '1's so I could view it and verify that the mask was read correctly.

```c
void TestPlayerShip(char * filename,char * textfn) {
    FILE * fmask;
    int error = fopen_s(&fmask, filename, "rb");
    error = fread_s(plmask, sizeof(plmask), sizeof(plmask), 1, fmask);
    fclose(fmask);
    error = fopen_s(&fmask, textfn, "wt");
    for (int i = 0; i < 24; i++) {
        fprintf_s(fmask, "Rotation %d\n", i);
        for (int y = 0; y < 64; y++)
        {
            for (int x = 0; x < 64; x++) {
                byte b = plmask[i][y][x];
                fprintf(fmask, "%d", b);
            }
            fprintf(fmask, "\n");
        }
        fprintf(fmask, "\n");
    }
    fclose(fmask);
}
```

That's where the mask image earlier came from.

I also created a more generic version of this function TestMask which lets you specify the size (it assumes square), number of rotations, a pointer to the mask and the target text file.

There's two text files in the chapter 38 zip file asteroid.txt and pl.txt each showing the 24 rotations.

So going forward we'll use these masks in the game for the collision detection.

Resource Manager

Another side note. If this was a commercial game, I'd create and use a resource manager for loading data and decompressing it. For example the masks are full of 0 and 1 bytes and compress very well.

The largest mask for the 24 x 280x280 asteroids is a 1.9 MB file but compresses with Winzip down to 30KB. So instead of having lots of files as we do, we'd have just one big file containing images, sounds, masks etc.

The program would at the right time request a particular resource with a call to extract sound etc.

Files for this chapter.

The zip file containing everything is genmask_ch38.zip.

Chapter 39. Detecting Collisions Part 2

Now that we have the masks, we can add them to the game. I did consider adding the genmask code to the program but we only need the masks to be generated once. So first we have to define them and then load them.

```c
char plmask[24][64][64];
char a1mask[24][280][280];
char a2mask[24][140][140];
char a3mask[24][70][70];
char a4mask[24][35][35];
char bmask[1][3][3];
char * maskErrorFile;
int LoadMask(char * filename, int size, int number, char * mask) {
    FILE * fmask;
    maskErrorFile = filename;
    int sizeofmask = size * size*number;
    int error = fopen_s(&fmask, filename, "rb");
    if (error != 0) return 0;
    int numread = fread_s(mask, sizeofmask, sizeofmask, 1, fmask);
    fclose(fmask);
    return numread == 1 ? 1 : 0;
}
```

```
// Load all masks if any return 0 then failed to load so exit
int LoadMasks() {
    maskErrorFile = NULL;
    if (!LoadMask("bullet.msk", 3, 1, &blmask[0][0][0])) return 0; // bullet
    if (!LoadMask("playership.msk", 64, 24, &plmask[0][0][0])) return 0; // playership
    if (!LoadMask("am1.msk", 280, 24, &a1mask[0][0][0])) return 0;
    if (!LoadMask("am2.msk", 140, 24, &a2mask[0][0][0])) return 0;
    if (!LoadMask("am3.msk", 70, 24, &a3mask[0][0][0])) return 0;
    return LoadMask("am4.msk", 35, 24, &a4mask[0][0][0]);
}
```

Should any masks fail to load, the maskErrorFile variable has the name of the failed file.

Checking for Collisions

We need to check for a collision when

- The player's ship moves.
- An asteroid moves.
- A bullet moves.

We really need this to be fast, every time that object moves we need to see if it's near any other objects.

Each object has y,x coordinates and a size.

To check if two objects O1 and O2 overlap, we add an SDL_Rect called r to each object (player ship, asteroid and bullet) with x,y, width and height. This is the bounding square for each object that you can see when the debugFlag == 1.

Storing positions twice is a little bit inefficient as we've already got float x and y positions but it's for speed. When the object is initialised, the r.w and r.h fields are set. Every time the object moves, the r.y and r.x fields are updated.

Why do we have both float and int x and y? *The float versions are so we can have small velocities <1 in any direction and keep adding them. The int coordinates are for the exact points and we'll need those for calculating overlaps.*

Intersecting rectangles with SDL

Now there's an SDL function SDL_IntersectRect that tells us if two object's rectangles overlap.

The problem is, if there's theoretically up to 64 asteroids in play and 16 bullets plus the player's ship theoretically adding up to 81 objects.

We'll also later add 3 alien ships with 8 bullets each so that makes 64 + 16 + 1 + 3 + 24 = 108 objects.

To check each object against the other 108 is 108*107/2 = 5778 calls to SDL_IntersectRect. It's fast but when you do that 60 times a second, it will grind the computer to a halt. I tried it and it was so slow the game ran at 4 frames per second!

We need to reduce this time; it doesn't make sense to check each one against all of them as they are never all going to be near each other.

Now in reality we wouldn't have 64 asteroids, that many would likely cover most screen pixels which would make the game kind of tough! (Understatement...!)

Reducing Collision Checks

We need a way to reduce the number of comparisons. Remember these comparisons are just to check if two objects are near enough that they might touch. **Then** we still have to do the pixel-perfect collision checks.

The scheme I devised starts by virtually splitting the screen area into cells each 64 x 64 pixels.

A screen size of 1024 x 768 divides neatly in 192 such cells (192 = 16 across x 12 down). Think of these cells as organized in this way on the next page.

In reality they are held in two dimensions with x is 0..15 and y from 0..11 but just bear with me and imagine each as a number 0-191. This is the calculation **cell number = y * 16 + x**.

Laid out starting from the top left (0) to the bottom right (191) it looks like this:

```
0,1,2,3......15
  16, 17, 18...31
  32..........47
  ..
  177,178.....191
```

When each object moves, it calls a function to add it to the cells that it covers. In each cell we'll have an int called numobjects and an array of pointers called ptrs.

```
struct CELL {
    ptrarray ptrs;
    int numobjects;
};
struct CELL cells[CELLX][CELLY];
```

I'll explain why ptrarray ptrs is used for a bit later but for now it's just the typedef name for an array of pointers.

Objects and cells

The biggest object in the game is a type 0 asteroid at 280 x 280 pixels. That will sit across 25, 30 or 36 cells. Because 280 is 4.375 * 64 i.e. it needs at least five cells in both directions.

If the coordinates are an exact multiple of 64 say 64,64 then it touches five cells across (cells 0-4) and five cells down (0,16,32,48 and 64) touching 25 in total.

if it were situated at 52,52 then horizontally there would be 12 pixels in cell 0, 64 in cells 1,2,3,4 and 12 pixels in cell 5. (4 x 64 + 2 x 12 = 280). So that would be touching 6 cells across and down, 36 in total.

Smaller objects such as the player ship which is 64 x 64 pixels touches either one cell if the x,y coordinates are an exact multiple of 64,or 2 or 4 cells. Even the humble bullet at 3 x 3 will spend most of its time in one cell but will occasionally cross cells so could be touching two or even four cells now and then.

Why do we add an object to cells?

Because it reduces the number of comparisons to a much smaller and manageable number. We just need to look in each cell. If numobjects is two or more then there's a possible collision. If it's 0 or 1 then there's no way a collision can take place.

Adding an object to a cell?

Now what do I mean by adding an object to a cell? I mean we add a pointer to that object into the cell's ptrs array. Any cell could in theory have all 108 objects in it.

It's really, really, really unlikely but by allocating enough memory for 108 pointers in each cell, we're covered. That's in one cell and there are 192 cells in total.

The first part of three phases of collision detection is to add moving objects into the cells array.

Phase two is to process all the cells with two or more objects and call SDL_IntersectRect on all pairs of objects in that cell. Finally phase three does pixel perfect checking on all pairs that overlapped.

Processing Cells

Now each frame there's a good chance that many cells will have nothing or maybe one object in them, in which case we do nothing in that cell.

We could just do a double loop with 16 x 12 = 192 times checking the numobjects in each cell. But we're smarter than that! For a little bit more memory we can improve on it.

We declare an array of 192 pairs of ints that I call cellList[192] and this is cleared each frame. When we add an object to a cell, if that is the first object added to that cell, we add the cell's coordinates to the cellList.

So after we've added all the objects into the cells they're covering we have a list of cells that have two or more objects in.

We can then loop through each of those cells in cellList and for those with two or more objects in, we check the objects using SDL_IntersectRect to see which ones overlap.

Checking Each Cell

If we have n objects, we need to call SDL_IntersectRect $n * (n-1)/2$ times. Let me explain how I get this. Say we have five objects in a cell, numbered 0-4. Let's put them in a table where a * means we do a check.

```
  0 1 2 3 4
0 . * * * *
1 . . * * *
2 . . . * *
3 . . . . *
4 . . . . .
```

It's triangle shaped because we don't check objects against themselves nor do we check them twice.

So we call SDL_IntersectRect for 0 down and 1 across, but not for 1 down and 0 across etc. So for n = 5 there are 10 checks to do = (5 x 4/2). For 6 there are 15 checks and so on.

For n objects, it's n * (n-1)/2 checks needed.

Objects in a Cell

I've used the word object to mean anything moving that can hit anything else. so it can be a player ship, an asteroid or a bullet but not an explosion. Explosions animate but they remain fixed where they are until they've cycled through all the frames. Then they vanish.

I've now moved the fields around in the asteroid, player and bullet structs so they all start with these same three fields.

```
SDL_Rect r;
int type; // 0
int active;
```

and created a struct in its own right, called firstpart.

```
struct firstpart {
    SDL_Rect r;
    int type;
    int active;
};
typedef struct firstpart * pfirstpart;
```

Why would I have a struct that is the same as the start of the three structs? Because it's easier to manipulate them with it; we only need to access the "first part" of each structure because the fields are the same regardless of whether its a bullet, asterpoid or playership.

All three types start with the same layout, so we can cast them to a pointer to a firstpart. As one of the fields is type, we can cast back to the correct type when we need to.

The reason I use firstpart is because the object structs are different sizes. Remember a pointer has both the address of an object in memory and the type of that object. The type tells the C compiler how big the object is.

So the ptr list in a cell has pointers to all objects in this cell irrespective of their type. I've also defined a typedef (another name for a type) for a pointer to a firstpart called pfirstpart.

Personal opinion. Some C programmers don't like using types like pfirstpart because it eliminates most of the *. I find it makes it easier to read source code without so many *. But please use whichever way you prefer.

Adding a pointer into a list of pointers in a cell.

To add a pointer into a list of pointers for a given cell is this lovely bit of code.

```
void AddPointerToCell(int x, int y, pfirstpart objectptr) {
   int numobjects = cells[x][y].numobjects;
   if (!numobjects) { // 1st time cell added to so add to cellList
      cellList[numcells].x = x;
      cellList[numcells++].y = y;
   }
   cells[x][y].ptrs[numobjects] = objectptr;
   cells[x][y].numobjects++;
```

}

Let me break it down line by line. The first line in the function gets the number of objects already added into this cell in this frame. If it's 0 then it's the first and we add the x and y coords of this cell to the cellList.

We always copy the object pointer into the ptrs array in the cell and increment the numobjects there.

Again a personal preference, some people prefer an explicit increment so the if would look like this below instead. Feel free to use whichever you are happiest with. I like the postincrement.

cellList[numcells++].y = y;

This sets cellist[numcells].y = y then increments numcells.

But this is it with an explicit increment.

```
if (!numobjects) { // 1st time cell added to so add to cellList
   cellList[numcells].x = x;
   cellList[numcells].y = y;
   numcells++;
}
```

How many cells does an object cover?

When we move an Asteroid, or any other object we have to figure out how many cells it needs to be added to.

The function AddObjectToCells does this. You just pass into it a pointer to an object (pFirstpart), it extracts the location and size and then loops through adding itself to those cells.

When I first wrote this it didn't have the two ifs and crashed when objects were half off the screen.

```
void AddObjectToCells(pfirstpart objectptr) {
   int x = objectptr->r.x;
   int y = objectptr->r.y;
   int h = objectptr->r.h;
   int w = objectptr->r.w;
   int cellx = x / CELLSIZE;
   int celly = y / CELLSIZE;
   int endcellx = (x + w) / CELLSIZE;
   int endcelly = (y + h) / CELLSIZE;
   if (endcellx >= CELLX) endcellx = CELLX-1;
   if (endcelly >= CELLY) endcelly = CELLY-1;
   for (int ix = cellx; ix <= endcellx; ix++)
      for (int iy = celly; iy < endcelly; iy++)
         AddPointerToCell(ix, iy, objectptr);
}
```

As always the uppercase CELLSIZE means it's a #define declared value. I added these #defines to the program.

```
#define SCREENWIDTH 1024
#define SCREENHEIGHT 768
#define CELLSIZE 64
#define CELLY SCREENHEIGHT/CELLSIZE
#define CELLX SCREENWIDTH/CELLSIZE
```

Remember a #define defines text that is substituted just before the compiler compiles. So it does the divisions 1024/64 and 768/64 and CELLY will be 16 and CELLX 12.

If you ever change SCREENWIDTH or SCREENHEIGHT then the preprocessor part of the compiler will recompute CELLY and CELLX.

Pointers and arrows

In a struct you access the members by using a dot. You've seen that in the function AddPointerToCell a page or two back.

int numobjects = cells[x][y].numobjects;

But when we use a pointer to a struct you have to use an arrow -> instead.

int x = objectptr->r.x;

If we had a variable declared as a struct firstpart then you'd access the x variable (in r) with the . Anything accessing fields of a struct via a pointer always use the -> instead.

This is a made up example, not part of the game.

struct firstpart fp;
int x = fp.r.x;
int y = objectptr->r.y;

Here's a reminder of the first line of AddObjectToCells, the function's signature.

void AddObjectToCells(pfirstpart objectptr)

Below is a call to AddObjectToCells complete with a cast to convert it to a pointer to firstpart (pfirstpart).

AddObjectToCells((pfirstpart)&bullets[i]);

Because we're passing in a pointer, it expects an address. We get the address of a variable with & so &bullets[i] returns the address **of the struct in the array bullets at index i**.

That's a pointer to a bullet struct, but the function expects a pfirstpart so the cast just tells the compiler that the pointer passed in is a pfirstpart.

Back to the Cells

At the start of each GameLoop I've added a call to ClearCellList() which clears cellList and cells. It calls memset which very rapidly writes the value (0) to every byte. The number of bytes to write to cellist is got by calling sizeof(cellist).

The numcells variable is also cleared here.

```
void ClearCellList() {
   memset(cellList, 0, sizeof(cellList));
   memset(cells, 0, sizeof(cells));
   numcells = 0;
}
```

I was curious how long it takes to clear these memory locations each frame. We are doing a lot of things and an understanding of how long each takes is important. Remember at 60 fps to move everything and draw it to off-screen VRAM it must take less than 16 milliseconds per frame.

Timing ClearCellList

The build-in function memset() clears a block of memory at a specified address and size using very fast code.

The cells object is just under 80K in size and cellList is 192 pairs of ints which is 8 x 192 = 1536 bytes. Each cell has 108 pointers plus one int so that's 109 x 4 bytes = 436 and there are 192 of them.

So that's 436 x 192 = 83,712 bytes + 1536 = 85,248 bytes in total.

Out of curiosity, I used the timer calls to see how long ClearCellList takes. On my PC it's approximately 5 microseconds; it's a useful thing to know. Here's how I did the timing.

First I added a global variable timebuff.

```
char timebuff[20];
```

Then at the start of GameLoop added these variables.

```
stopWatch start;
double totalTime;
totalTime = 0.0;
int counter=0;
```

Then after the CheckPause in the While ProcessEvents in GameLoop, I added this code.

```
startTimer(&start);
ClearCellList();
stopTimer(&start);
totalTime += getElapsedTime(&start)*1000000;
counter++;
if (counter == 60) {
   sprintf_s(timebuff, sizeof(timebuff)-1,"%f5.2", totalTime / counter);
   counter = 0;
   totalTime = 0.0;
}
```

Note this adds the 60 times together then divides by counter (= 60) to get an average. Time is in seconds and being a very small number I multiplied it by a million to get microseconds.

Finally in the RenderEverything() function I added this just before the call to SDL_RenderPresent. Remember this "flips" between two different memory blocks that is displayed on screen. So you have to print text etc., render graphics before this.

```
TextAt(20, HEIGHT - 200, timebuff);
```

I've left the timing code in the source but commented out. There's no code for this chapter. I'll spring it all on you after the end of chapter 42.

Chapter 40. Detecting Collisions Part 3

Now that we've the CellList and Cells populated each frame, we call CheckCollisions() in the GameLoop to see what has hit what.

This will still only be the rough collision of the bounding boxes using SDL_IntersectRect hit, not the pixel perfect collision that I've promised you. We'll get to that shortly.

I added a call to CheckCollisions() in GameLoop() after everything has moved. We use the CellList to check all the Cells with potential collisions.

I haven't done Overlap yet but we do know that we will need to pass the two objects and the rect that is populated by the SDL_IntersectRect call.

The CheckCollisions function looks through the numcells elements in cellList to find those cells with 1 or more objects added.

If there are more than one object, it calls CheckAllObjects with the coordinates (x,y) of the cell.

```
void CheckCollisions() {
    for (int i = 0; i < numcells; i++) {
        int x = cellList[i].x;
        int y = cellList[i].y;
        if (cells[x][y].numobjects > 1) {
            CheckAllObjects(x, y);
        }
    }
}

// Double loop to see if any pairs of objects in this overlap.
void CheckAllObjects(int x, int y) {
    struct Cell * c = &cells[x][y];
    SDL_Rect rect;
```

```
    for (int index1=0;index1<c->numobjects;index1++)
        for (int index2 = index1 + 1; index2 < c->numobjects; index2++) {
            if (SDL_IntersectRect(&c->ptrs[index1]->r, &c->ptrs[index2]->r, &rect)) {
                // if (overlap(&c->ptrs[index1],&c->ptrs[index2],&rect) {
                // kill both objects...
                // }
            }
        }
}
```

The nested for-loops in CheckAllObjects makes the 'triangle' happen. Let's look at this code so you can see how it works.

```
for (int index1=0;index1<c.numobjects;index1++)
    for (int index2 = index1 + 1; index2 < c.numobjects; index2++)
```

Let's try it out with five objects in this cell. (x,y) means compare object x with object y.

index1 = 0. index2 goes from 1 to 4 and does **(0,1), (0,2), (0,3)** and **(0,4)**
index1 = 1. index2 goes from 2 to 4 and does **(1,2), (1,3), (1,4)**
index1 = 2. index2 goes from 3 to 4 and does **(2,3), (2,4)**
index1 = 3. index2 goes from 4 to 4 and does **(3,4)**

And that's all the ten combinations of 5 objects. Remember that's 5 x (5-1) / 2 = 10 possible overlaps.

After a long chapter 39, I kept this one deliberately short. Don't worry, there will be longer ones soon enough!

Now before we do the fourth chapter (42) on pixel perfect collision detection, here is a chapter on passing parameters into functions. Trust me, it's highly relevant.

Chapter 41. Passing Parameters into functions.

Since I introduced pointers, I've increasingly made use of the & operator. Remember &variable gives you the address of a variable in memory.

int a = 1;
int * pa = &a;

Here I've declared an int variable a and initialized it to 1. I've also created a pointer variable called pa which has been initialised with the address of a.

If a is at address 1000 then pa holds the value 1000. Remember that a pointer variable just holds an address.

Now when you pass values into a function, the value passed in is copied in. You can't pass a value out of a function via the function parameters but a function can return a value.

But what if you passed a pointer variable in? Take a look at this program. What value will be printed out? This is program pointer2.c in the examples folder.

```
#include <stdio.h>
void inc(int * pvalue) {
    *pvalue = *pvalue + 1;
}
int main()
{
   int a = 1;
   int * pa = &a;
   inc(pa);
     printf("%i\n",a);
}
```

The answer is 2. The inc function accepts a pointer to an int. Outside the function we have pa which has the address of a. At the start a has the value 1.

We call inc() and pass pa into it. The address of a (say it's 1000) is passed in and assigned to pvalue which is also a pointer to an int.

At this point we have two variables (pa outside the function) and pvalue inside it, both with the address of a which we know is 1000. *pvalue means the value stored at the address held in pvalue. As the address is 1000, we know it contains the value 1.

If it helps, when we talk about the variable a, remind yourself that a is nothing more than a name for a location in memory. The declaration of a tells the compiler that it holds an int.

So *pvalue = *pvalue + 1 just adds 1 to the value stored in location 1000. When it gets to the printf, it prints out the value in memory at 1000 and you get 2.

Using ++ with pointers

You can shorten *pvalue = *pvalue + 1 with ++ but you have to be careful. Which of these is correct?

(*pa)++

*pa++;

Answer: the first one. It increments the value at the address in pa. The second one increments pa, the address. As it's an int *, this means it points to an address one int (=4 bytes) further on.

If pa was 1000 then after *pa++, pa would have the value 1004 because an int is four bytes.

If you have a pointer to a byte or char, both of which are 1 byte types then adding 1 to the pointer will change it to 1001.

Why are pointers so important?

In C it is possible but not very good programming practice to have all variables held globally.

Why is it bad? Because your data is accessible from any part of the program and in large programs, some code far away might alter your data without you realising it.

It's a good programming practice to limit access to variables.

In chapter 40, I put in a stub for the overlap function. This function passes in the two firstparts of the objects whose bounding boxes overlap and gives back a SDL_Rect that says where they overlapped.

If we passed in a copy of those firstparts, instead of a pointer, it would be slightly slower but would not change the active flag in the real object, only the copy.

Passing in pointers lets the overlap function directly access object data in memory and change it. Here it is again.

```
void CheckAllObjects(int x, int y) {
   struct Cell * c = &cells[x][y];
   SDL_Rect rect;
   for (int index1=0;index1<c->numobjects;index1++)
      for (int index2 = index1 + 1; index2 < c->numobjects; index2++) {
         if (SDL_IntersectRect(&c->ptrs[index1]->r, &c->ptrs[index2]->r, &rect)) {
            if (Overlap(c->ptrs[index1], c->ptrs[index2], &rect)) {
               DestroyObject(c->ptrs[index1]);
               DestroyObject(c->ptrs[index2]);
            }
         }
      }
}
```

The first line assigns the address of the cell defined by the x and y coordinates. There's 192 cells but we're just looking at one of them in this function, the one defined by the x, y parameters passed in to the CheckAllObjects function.

struct Cell * c = &cells[x][y];

This sets c **to point to** the cell.

Each cell has two fields: numobjects, a count of the objects in this cell and ptrs, an array of pointers to the objects.

Because c is a pointer, it uses c-> to access the fields. The first parameter to pass into SDL_IntersectRect is this.

&c->ptrs[index1]->r

That is confusing. Read it as **the address of the r field of the index1'th element in the ptrs array, in the cell pointed to by c**. Although the & is on the c it applies to the r value.

It gets the address of r in **c->ptrs[index1]->r**

So inside the double loop, it calls SDL_IntersectRect and passes in pointers to both objects and the address of somewhere to hold the overlap rectangle that is passed back from SDL_IntersectRect. I'll say more about that rectangle in the next chapter.

If I hadn't used pointers and instead did this:

```
struct Cell c = &cells[x][y];
```

It would have copied 432 bytes from cells[x][y] into c. Now 432 bytes isn't a lot by itself but say ten of these 60 times a second adds up to 600 x 432 bytes = 259,200 bytes.

It makes no sense to copy 432 bytes if by using a pointer we can just copy four bytes or 2400 bytes a second. Plus you still have to pass in pointers with SDL_IntersectRect.

When to use & and when not to

In the CheckAllObjects these two lines can be really confusing.

```
if (SDL_IntersectRect(&c->ptrs[index1]->r, &c->ptrs[index2]->r, &rect))
{
    if (Overlap(c->ptrs[index1], c->ptrs[index2], &rect)) {
```

In the call to SDL_IntersectRect I use & to pass in the parameters but in the call to Overlap I don't. Why is this?

If you look at what's passed into SDL_IntersectRect, the first two parameters passed in are the addresses of rects. The r parameter in firstpart is an SDL_Rect.

If you remember struct firstpart:

```
struct firstpart {
    SDL_Rect r;
    int type;
    int active;
};
```

Now select SDL_Rect with the mouse then right click on it and click Goto Definition on the popup menu. It should open the file SDL_Rect.h and you should see this.

```
typedef struct SDL_Rect
{
    int x, y;
    int w, h;
} SDL_Rect;
```

So our r field in firstparam contains 4 ints (x,y,w and h). That means it's 16 bytes in size. Whereas the pointer &c->ptrs[index1]->r is only 4 bytes in size. It's quicker to pass in two pointers (8 bytes) than two 16-byte structs (32 bytes).

However the Overlap function actually takes two pointers so that's why we pass them in directly.

The idea is to use & when there's a large object, so you pass in the address of the object rather than copy the object's bytes.

You should write code to minimize the amount of data to copy. Even though it is fast at copying bytes, on my PC about five microseconds for 80Kb is copying about 16KB per microsecond.

At 60 frames per second that means roughly 16 milliseconds (16,000 microseconds) is available per frame. Setting against that, the five microseconds is a very small part of it but I'd still rather write lean, fast code.

The next chapter completes collision detection.

Chapter 42. Detecting Collisions Part 4

In the SDL_IntersectRect call the 3rd parameter is a pointer to a SDL_Rect and the call populates this rect , i.e. if the two objects locations overlap it returns a rectangle at the intersection of the two objects. It's the key to pixel accurate collisions.

Imagine two bounding boxes overlapping, you can see that the area of overlap will only ever be rectangular or square. Every pixel in that intersection rectangle is a pixel out of both objects.

Here is a very crude way of showing this. Imagine two small shapes. To make them clearer I've used 1s and 2s to show the solid pixels; these correspond to 1 bytes in the masks. The dots represent blank pixels or 0 in the masks.

```
................
..111.....2222..
.11111...2....2.
.11111...2....2.
..1111....2...2.
..111......222..
................
```

The 2 shape now moves three pixels left.

```
. . . . . . . . . . . .
..111..2222..
.111112....2.
.111112....2.
..1111.2...2.
..111...222..
. . . . . . . . . . . .
```

Now the 2 shape moves one pixel left and they overlap shown by the rectangle. Where the 1 and 2 pixels overlap I've shown an X.

```
. . . . . . . . . . . .
..111.2222..
.1111X....2.
.1111X....2.
..1112...2.
..111..222..
. . . . . . . . . . . .
```

What we do get back from SDL_IntersectRect is that rectangle; 7 vertical by 1 wide rect with x,y position and width=1 height=7. The seven pixels running vertically are ..XX1.. Ignore the 1 though, only the X count.

We know the coordinates and size of the two overlapping objects. We can thus calculate the offset of the overlapping pixels relative to each of the object's masks and get a 1 or 0 back for each of the seven pixels.

You can see that the vertical column is the 5th column in the 1 object and 0th column in the 2 object.

From the 2 mask we get back the 0th column which reading vertically is ..11... and from the 1 object mask column 0 we get ..111.. If we "binary and" these bits together we get 0011000. Or 00XX000 in the image above.

Forgotten binary-and? Have another read of binary-and.

As soon as a 1 pixel (an X in the image) is found from the anding, we return true and exit. There are no more checks. The first collision removes any need to do more checking.

When we have a collision we have to blow up both objects. I've created a function DestroyObject which is called once for each object, passing in the underlying firstpart pointer.

The Overlap function

This is the function that takes pointers to two objects. It then processes the rect from SDL_Intersect and checks if the corresponding masks' pixels touch. If they do it returns the point using the bangx and bangy pointers.

```
int Overlap(pfirstpart object1, pfirstpart object2, SDL_Rect * rect,int * bangx,int * bangy) {
    int y = rect->y;
    int x = rect->x;
    int w = rect->w;
    int h = rect->h;
    int y1 = object1->r.y;
    int x1 = object1->r.x;
```

```
    int y2 = object2->r.y;
    int x2 = object2->r.x;
    int dir1 = object1->type == tBullet ? 0: object1->rotdir;
    int dir2 = object2->type == tBullet ? 0: object2->rotdir;
    int size1 = object1->r.h;
    int size2 = object2->r.h;
     pbyte pm1 = GetMask(object1->type, object1->rotdir, size1);
     pbyte pm2 = GetMask(object2->type, object2->rotdir, size2);
    int oy1 = y - y1;
    int oy2 = y - y2;
    int ox1 = x - x1;
    int ox2 = x - x2;
    pm1 += (oy1 *size1) + ox1;
    pm2 += (oy2 *size2) + ox2;
    for (int iy = 0; iy < h; iy++)
      {
      pbyte pl1 = pm1;
      pbyte pl2 = pm2;
      *bangy = iy + y;
      for (int ix = 0; ix < w; ix++) {
         *bangx = ix + x;
         if (*pl1++ & *pl2++) {
            return 1;
         }
      }
      pm1 += size1;
      pm2 += size2;
    }
    return 0;
}
```

Explanation of Overlap

The first four lines extract y,x,w and h from the overlapped rectangle. We'll use those in the two for- loops. The next four lines get the y and x coordinates for the two objects.

We now get the (rotation) directions with these lines:

```
int dir1 = object1->type == tBullet ? 0 : object1->rotdir;
int dir2 = object2->type == tBullet ? 0 : object2->rotdir;
```

If object1's type equals tBullet then the value is 0 otherwise the value is its rotation dir.

Type 1 is a bullet and doen't have rotations so there's no rotdir, just return 0 for that. For everything else we return the object's rotdir. This is a value between 0 and 23 for the player's ship and the asteroids.

Now we extract the size. All objects of the same type have the same width or height so we can use r.h or r.w. We need the sizes for the mask and indexing into the mask.

Next we get the two masks. We have several different size masks so I'm using a byte pointer to index in them. The typedef pbyte is easier to read than byte * although it means exactly the same.

Because it points to a byte when you add 1 to the pointer address, it increases it by 1. If it was an int ptr, adding 1 to the pointer would increase the address by 4.

The GetMask function returns a pointer to the first byte of a mask, and if it's not a bullet, this is a pointer to the first byte of the correct rotation mask.

The GetMask function takes the object's type, rotation and size. It only needs size for asteroids, and rotation for asteroids and the player ship. Because the masks are all different sizes, the returned values have all to be cast to pbyte.

The pointers pm1 and pm2 are pointers to the two masks. But we only need the parts of the masks that correspond to the overlapped rectangle. Here the * means multiply.

pm1 += (oy1 * size1) + ox1;
pm2 += (oy2 * size2) + ox2;

This adjusts positions Pm1 and Pm2 to point to the correct part in each of the two masks; the part that corresponds to the overlap rectangle. These use ox1, oy1 and oy2, ox2. These are offsets from the top left point of each object (y1, x1 and y2,x2) to the top left of the overlap rectangle y,x.

The offsets can only be zero or positive, never negative. Don't believe me? Draw two overlapping rectangles, call them 1 and 2. Where they overlap we call the top left point of the overlap y,x and the top left point of rectangle 1 is y1,x1 and the top left overlap of rectangle 2 is y2,x2. The offsets are y1-y,x1-x for rectangel 1 and y2-y,x2-x for rectangle 2.

So now we do two nested loops, looking at the appropriate bytes. The iy loop iterates through every row in the overlapped section. At the start of each row, the two pointers pl1 and pl2 are copied from pm1 and pm2. These two variables pm1 and pm2 point to the start of the overlap in each successive row in each mask.

Then if (*pl1++ & pl2++) does its magic with a binary-and. Each byte in the mask is a 0 or 1 and only when both are 1 does the collision occur.

Think of a bullet with a 3 x 3 shape. The mask looks like this.

010
111
010

If this is overlapped by two pixels (say into the right side of as an asteroid) then we only have to compare the first two bytes of each row. If this is object1 then pl1 fisrt points to the top left 0 then the 1 next to it.

At this point we are finished with the first row and add 3 to pm1 so that it points to the first byte in the 2nd row. (Which is 1) then the next byte which is also 1.

Let's have another diagram. We have two objects who for simplicity are 8 x 8 and 4 x 4 in size. We'll call them 1 and 2. These are the masks.

```
.111111.
11111111
11111111    ....
11111111    .22.
11111111    .22.
11111111    ....
11111111
11111111
.111111.
```

After they collide, it looks like this. The 1 column of the 4 x 4 overlaps with the 7th column (last one) of the 8 x 8.

```
.111111.
11111111
11111111..
1111111X2.
1111111X2.
11111111
11111111
.111111.
```

If we take the 1 shape at y=0,x=0 to keep things simple then the 2 shape is at y=2, x = 6.

The overlap rect is at y = 2 and x =6 and has h = 4 and w = 2. So the iy loop is from y=2 to y=5 and the ix loop from x=6 to x=7.

The two collision pixels we are checking are at these locations. (3,7) and (4,7)

Now we subtract the address (top left of each object)

Object 1 at 0,0 means we look at pixels (3,7) and (4,7) in object 1. Both are 1s.

Object 2 at 2,6 means we look at (1,2) and (2,2) in object 2. These are both 1s.

So we now have a collision. In fact after we compared 3,7 with 1,2 and got a collision we immediately exit.

Destroying Objects

When two objects touch, we call DestroyObject for each object.

```
void PlayerLosesALife() {
    Player.lives--;
    if (Player.lives > 0) {
        InitPlayer(Player.lives);
        InitAsteroids();
        InitBullets();
        InitExplosions();
    }
    // Handle last life lost in GameLoop()
}
void DestroyObject(pfirstpart object) {
    switch (object->type) {
    case 0: // asteroid
        DestroyThisAsteroid((struct asteroid *)object); break;
    case 1: // bullet
        object->active = 0;
        break;
    case 2: // player only use Player no need to pass in object
        PlayerLosesALife();
        break;
    }
}
```

The InitPlayer call seems a bit odd. It just sets Player.Lives to the value passed in which is the value it already has.

We've decremented it at the start of PlayerLosesALife() and it's just one of several Player fields that have to be initialised in this routine. When Player.Lives reaches 0, we don't do the init stuff. Instead we let it drop out of the GameLoop.

```
      while (ProcessEvents())
      {
         CheckPause();
         if (!paused) {
            if (Player.lives == 0) break;
```

I've used break, not return so it drops out of the while (ProcessEvents()) loop instead of returning from GameLoop. If there's any other game cleanup processing to be done, we do it at the end of GameLoop.

How much processing time does it take?

After I added the SDL_IntersectRect calls, I also added showing the overlap rectangles as green wireframes. As two objects move closer and the green rectangles form, I disabled the explosions to see how long the overlap code was taking. So objects could move through each other.

What was particularly interesting was when two large asteroids overlapped, everything ground to a halt and the frame rate dropped from 60 to 4. That was over 70,000 calls to Overlap per frame = 70,000 x 60 = over four million calls per second!

Of course in normal play as soon as they touch, they explode so this was way beyond the worst case. But it just shows how important it is to do things as fast as possible.

Viewing the overlap pixels

To satisfy myself that the collision detection was working correctly I decided to turn off the explosion and show the overlap as green pixels.

The first #define is SHOWOVERLAP and it'll be commented out. Uncomment it. Comment it out means put // at the start of the line. Uncomment it means just remove those //.

It's very easy, in the Overlap function you'll see two blocks of lines inside a #IFDEF SHOWOVERLAP

```
#ifdef SHOWOVERLAP
   SDL_SetRenderDrawColor(renderer, 0, 0xff, 0, SDL_ALPHA_OPAQUE);
#endif
```

And

```
#ifndef SHOWOVERLAP
        if (*pl1++ & *pl2++) {
            return 1; // hit!
    }
#else
        if (*pl1++ & *pl2++) {
            if (object1->type == 0 || object2->type == 0) { // comment this out- it'll show all overlaps but run very very slowly
                SDL_RenderDrawPoint(renderer, bangx, bangy);
        //}
    }
#endif
```

Whenever anything moves over the player ship, it'll display green pixels at the collision points as the picture below shows. Don't forget to comment out SHOWOVERLAP to have it playing correctly!

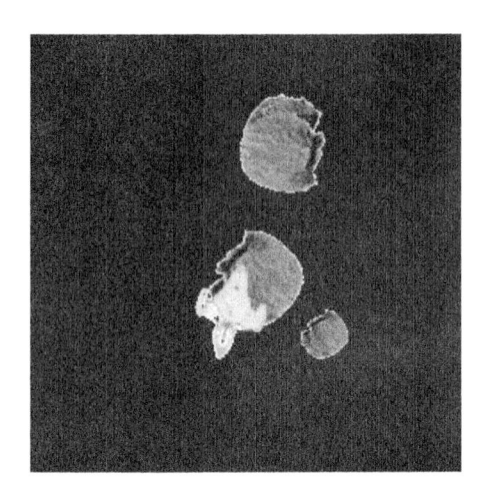

In the second block above that starts if (object1-> type == 0), if you comment this if line out and the matching } on the line after the SDL_RenderDrawPoint, you'll see all collisions not just the player ship but when asteroids overlap it will run very **very** slowly.

Files for this chapter.

The zip file containing everything is asteroids_ch42.zip.

Chapter 43. Ever Wondered about if (!value)

The previous chapters on collision detection have been pretty heavy so in this one, as a bit of light entertainment I'm settling the question of which is the best way to compare an int value against 0.

We've two contenders.

if (value == 0)

if (!value)

Arguably the first one is more explicit but after a while the second one becomes second nature so in that respect, it's a personal choice. But what about the code that's generated?

I wrote a short program to see what the compiler generates. This is program decnot.c in the examples folder

```
#include <stdio.h>
int value = 2;
void DecNot() {
    if (value == 0) return;
    value--;
}
void DecNot2() {
    if (!value) return;
    value--;
}
int main() {
    DecNot();
    DecNot2();
    printf("Value = %d", value);
}
```

When you compile this, first make sure it says Debug in the Standard toolbar and x86 and press F10 to start it running. It will stop on the first line of main.

Click Debug on the main menu then click on Windows in the Debug menu and on the second menu that pops up press Disassembly; it's one above the bottom of that menu.

You should now see a Disassembly listing in the editor. It's positioned at the start of main and shows the assembly instructions and machine code bytes for each line. You can step through as usual if you want. There's also a fair bit of extra code generated at the start and end of each function.

This is what the listing looks like on mine. You might see the same disassembled code as below but at different addresses. The addresses will change on subsequent debugs as well.

The first column is the address of the instruction in RAM or the line number (slightly indented) of the C code. The second column e.g. the first line starts B9 03 90 etc. is the C code instruction or the machine code values of the assembly instructions.

The 3rd column is the assembly language instruction (e.g. test) and the 4th column, any values like eax,eax in DecNot().

```
     15: int main() {
00E215D0 B9 03 90 E2 00       mov       ecx,offset _85527CF2_decnot@c (0E29003h)
00E215D5 E8 CF FB FF FF       call      @__CheckForDebuggerJustMyCode@4 (0E211A9h)
     16:     DecNot();
00E215DA A1 00 70 E2 00       mov       eax,dword ptr [value (0E27000h)]
     16:     DecNot();
00E215DF 85 C0                test      eax,eax
00E215E1 74 10                je        main+23h (0E215F3h)
00E215E3 83 C0 FF             add       eax,0FFFFFFFFh
00E215E6 A3 00 70 E2 00       mov       dword ptr [value (0E27000h)],eax
     17:     DecNot2();
00E215EB 74 06                je        main+23h (0E215F3h)
00E215ED 48                   dec       eax
00E215EE A3 00 70 E2 00       mov       dword ptr [value (0E27000h)],eax
     18:     printf("Value = %d", value);
00E215F3 50                   push      eax
00E215F4 68 30 5B E2 00       push      offset string "Value = %d" (0E25B30h)
00E215F9 E8 3E FA FF FF       call      _printf (0E2103Ch)
00E215FE 83 C4 08             add       esp,8
     19: }
00E21601 33 C0                xor       eax,eax
00E21603 C3                   ret
```

Here the DecNot and DecNot2 functions have been inlined into the main body; the compiler hasn't created separate routines just put the code in the main body. But you can see the two comparisons at addresses 00E215E1 and 00E125EB are identical.

In other words the compiler produces exactly the same code for both! Now if you mess around with the Optimize settings and compile in release mode, it might generate different code.

This chapter wasn't really about differences between two similar pieces of code but trying to show you other ways of looking at your program.

You don't need to write assembly language; that's the name for the instructions like **push ebx** that the disassembler generated. You might have been told that assembly language is quicker at running than the code that higher level languages like C produce. That is true but only if you know what you are doing. You have to be an expert to write it.

The experts who write C compilers program them to generate code from compiled C that will run faster most of the time than assembly code that you wrote!.

When checking to see what code is produced, I've found it best to do it in Debug mode. If you switch to release and do a full Rebuild the compiler will do lots of optimization and it can be a lot harder to see what's going on.

In the next chapter we'll look at some debugging tips.

Chapter 44. Some Debugging Tips

You might be tempted to think that all went smoothly and no bugs happened during development of this.

I had a few crashes along the way, the main one was the cell calculation went out of range when objects moved off screen. The y or x coordinates sometimes went negative, messed up the cell index calculation, corrupting the asteroids table.

Range checking code fixed that.

So when you code in C you will have to expect to do debugging. It goes with the territory. Here's a few tips.

More Logging

One way I found to help me was adding in a few debugging routines. In lib.c you'll see a few log routines in addition to LogError and LogError2.

```c
void l2(char * loc, char * msg) {
    fprintf_s(dbf, "%s,%s\n", loc, msg);
}
void l(char * loc) {
    fprintf_s(dbf, "%s\n", loc);
}
void ln(char * loc, char * msg, int n) {
    fprintf_s(dbf, "%s,%s,%s\n", loc, msg, sltoa(n));
}
void InitLogging(char * filename) {
    int error = fopen_s(&dbf, "biglog.txt", "wt");
}
void CloseLogging() {
    fclose(dbf);
}
```

These are declared in lib.h so they can be accessed from the main program file asteroids.c. Remember for functions in another C file, you define them there and declare them in the header (.h) file.

This is what lib.h looks like.

```
// Logging functions
void l(char * loc);
void l2(char * loc, char * msg);
void ln(char * loc, char * msg, int n);
char * sltoa(int n);
void InitLogging(char * filename);
void CloseLogging();
```

Opening and closing a Log file 60 times per second is a bad idea. So instead there's just one call to Initlogging() when the program starts and then a call to CloseLogging() when the program finishes.

Use these functions sparingly. Windows can easily write to a file 60 times per second but you can end up with a lot of text. Ideally you just need some if condition so that you call them sparingly perhaps when something goes out of bounds.

Show me the cells

I created this temporary function and added it in the GameLoop() before the RenderEverything() call. It puts green lines across the screen (Tholian web anyone<g>! Google it). It shows in each cell how many objects are in that cell. This caught two minor bugs.

```
void ShowCells() {
    SDL_SetRenderDrawColor(renderer, 0,0xff, 0, SDL_ALPHA_OPAQUE);
    for (int y = 0; y < CELLY; y++) {
```

```
        int y1 = y * 64;
        int y2 = y1 + 64;
        for (int x = 0; x < CELLX; x++) {
            int x1 = x * 64;
            int x2 = x1 + 64;
            SDL_RenderDrawLine(renderer, x1, y1, x2, y1); // horizontal
            SDL_RenderDrawLine(renderer, x1, y1, x1, y2); // horizontal
            TextAt(x1 + 10, y1 + 10, sltoa(cells[x][y].numobjects));
        }
    }
}
```

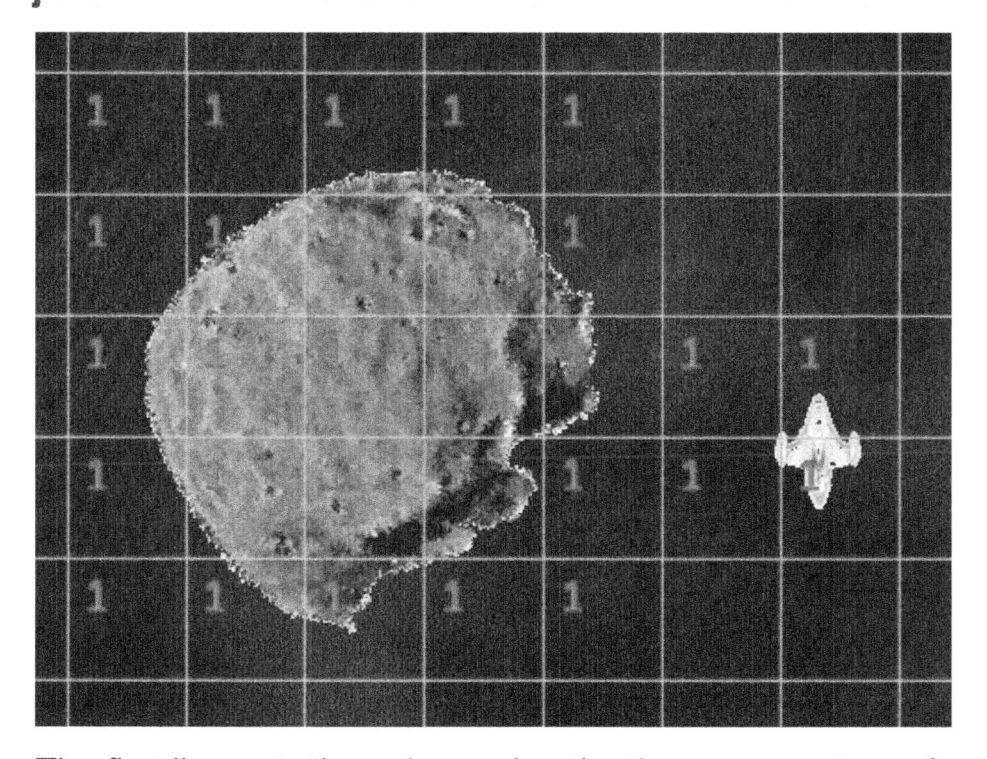

The first line sets the colour using the three parameters after renderer for red, green and blue. They can be hexadecimal 0xff or 255. The values above are 0,0xff,0 which is green.

The first bug was that asteroids and the player ship weren't being added to every cell under them. It was a simple bug. In AddObjectToCells, in the double loop at the end, I'd used < instead of <= so the last row and last column were skipped. This is the correct version.

```
for (int ix = cellx; ix <= endcellx; ix++)
   for (int iy = celly; iy <= endcelly; iy++)
      AddPointerToCell(ix, iy, objectptr);
```

Also it didn't show the correct number for bullets. I'd only called addobject to cells when the bullets moved. But they don't move every frame. So I just shifted the AddObjectToCell call outside the move code but still in the main for loop. if active part of the code.

```
void MoveBullets() {
    for (int i = 0; i< MAXBULLETS; i++) {
        struct bullet * pbullet = &bullets[i];
        if (pbullet->active && pbullet->countdown >0) {
            ... move code not shown here
            // even though a bullet doesn't move every frame, it still has to be added in to a cell every frame
            l2("Adding pointer bullets", sltoa(i));
            AddObjectToCells((pfirstpart)&bullets[i]);
        }
    }
}
```

When you want to stop the cells being displayed onscreen just comment out the ShowCells() at the end of GameLoop().

Files for this chapter.

The zip file containing everything is asteroids_ch44.zip.

Chapter 45. Improving the game

To be honest we haven't got a full game yet but most of the elements of it. When the player loses a life, the ship blows up and the level restarts and repeats until all three lives are lost.

A better way of handling losing a life is to set a flag and let the game run for another second or two doing explosions then start the next life. Just stopping game play the instant the life is lost is a poor experience for the player.

We need a timer. By which I mean a variable that is set to a value then decremented usually every frame. When it hits 0 it is reset to the initial value and this repeats.

I added a coolDown timer variable and set it to a value of 150 when the player's last ship is lost. Every time round the game loop it calls the CoolDown() function. The coolDown variable gets decremented when it's greater than 0. Once it reaches 0, it then calls PlayerLosesALife().

So after being destroyed, there's 2 and half seconds (150= 60 * 2.5) for explosions etc. Also the ship itself must explode, so I've added an explosion at the ship's x,y coordinates.

To make this work, I've also had to add if (!Player.active) return to both the MovePlayerShip() and DrawPlayerShip() functions.

Scores

The first addition is adding scores when you destroy an asteroid. That's 50 points. Alien ships will be 250 points but they're not going to be added for a few chapters yet.

To make things a little harder, you don't get 50 points for two asteroids colliding but only when you hit an asteroid with a bullet. Note I've tidied up code and this affects bullets and asteroids. So a little diversion first.

Previously I'd processed things like bullets and asteroids in arrays. They are still stored that way but if you look at say doFireBullet, it used to be this code.

```
void doFireBullet() {
    int index = -1;
    for (int i = 0; i<MAXBULLETS; i++) {
        if (bullets[i].ttl == 0) { // found a slot
            index = i;
            break;
        }
    }
    if (index == -1) return; // no free slots as all bullets in play
    int x = (int)round(Player.x + bulletx[Player.dir]);
    int y = (int)round(Player.y + bullety[Player.dir]);
    bullets[index].active = 1;
    bullets[index].type = tBullet;
    bullets[index].ttl = 120;
    bullets[index].x = x * 1.0f;
    bullets[index].y = y * 1.0f;
    bullets[index].r.x = (int)x;
    bullets[index].r.y = (int)y;
    bullets[index].r.h = 3;
    bullets[index].r.w = 3;
    bullets[index].timer = 3;
    bullets[index].countdown = 1;
    bullets[index].vx = Player.vx + thrustx[Player.dir] * 5;
    bullets[index].vy = Player.vy + thrusty[Player.dir] * 5;
    bullets[index].playerbullet = 1;
}
```

And now, I've simplified it slightly by using a pointer.

```
void DoFireBullet() {
    int index = -1;
    for (int i = 0; i<MAXBULLETS; i++) {
        if (bullets[i].ttl == 0) { // found a slot
            index = i;
            break;
        }
    }
    if (index == -1) return; // no free slots as all bullets in play
    PlayASound(CANNONSOUND);
    int x = (int)round(Player.x + bulletx[Player.dir]);
    int y = (int)round(Player.y + bullety[Player.dir]);
    struct bullet * pbullet = &bullets[index];
    pbullet->active = 1;
    pbullet->type = tBullet;
    pbullet->ttl = 120;
    pbullet->x = x * 1.0f;
    pbullet->y = y * 1.0f;
    pbullet->r.x = (int)x;
    pbullet->r.y = (int)y;
    pbullet->r.h = 3;
    pbullet->r.w = 3;
    pbullet->timer = 3;
    pbullet->countdown = 1;
    pbullet->vx = Player.vx + thrustx[Player.dir] * 5;
    pbullet->vy = Player.vy + thrusty[Player.dir] * 5;
    pbullet->playerbullet = 1;
}
```

There's one extra line that declares a pointer to a bullet and sets it to point to bullets[index].

```c
struct bullet * pbullet = &bullets[index];
```

I did it not just to make the program faster, though it might but to my mind it reads easier as there's less text. Both **bullets[index]** and **pbullet->** do the same; they access an element in the bullets array. I've also done this for asteroids.

Back to the score. We want to add 50 points only if a bullet hits an asteroid. So in CheckAllObjects, after the if Overlap, I added in this extra code.

```
if ((c->ptrs[index1]->type == tAsteroid && c->ptrs[index2]->type == tBullet) ||
    (c->ptrs[index2]->type == tAsteroid && c->ptrs[index1]->type == tBullet)) {
    score += 50;
}
```

That's all it takes. But keen observers might have spotted tAsteroid and tBullet. What are these?

They are a C feature called an **enum**. You take a list of values like (0,1,2) and give them names.

```
enum ObjectType {tAsteroid,tBullet,tPlayer};
```

The values are assigned by the C compiler with 0 first. So tPlayer is 2. However you are not forced to use that value. If you want 5 for tBullet and 10 for tPlayer then this you declare this.

```
enum ObjectType {tAsteroid,tBullet=5,tPlayer=10};
```

But lets jazz it up a bit. Some arcade games show the score next to or above the on-screen object that you destroyed and then animate it slightly.

So I'm going to add a new object; a textsprite. It is a bit of text, e.g. the 50 score and it puts it on screen just above the destroyed object. It won't collide so doesn't need to be a like a bullet, or asteroid. Here's the definition.

```
struct TextSprite {
    int x, y;
    int active;
    char message[10];
};
```

I'll use active as both the flag and a counter and it gets set to 75 in AddTextSprite. If a TextSprite object is active (i.e active >0) then each frame we decrement active counter and decrease the y field so it slowly move up the screen. If this takes it off screen then active is set immediately to 0.

I've also added an array for textsprites which as usual is defined by a #define value MAXTEXTSPRITES.

```
#define MAXTEXTSPRITES 10
struct TextSprite sprites[MAXTEXTSPRITES].
void AddTextSprite(int value, int x, int y) {
   int spriteindex = findFreeSprite();
   if (spriteindex == -1 || y <20) return;
   struct TextSprite * psprite = &sprites[spriteindex];
   psprite->x = x;
   psprite->y = y;
   psprite->active = 75;
   strcpy_s(psprite->message, sizeof(psprite->message), sltoa(value));
   numsprites++;
}
```

There's nothing really special in this except the use of a string. A C string is a block of chars in memory that ends with a 0 byte. In the third line, we have a pointer psprite to a sprite entry in the sprites array. The next three lines set x,y and active but the **strcpy_s** line is new.

The function **strcpy_s** is a built-in function that copies a text string. The **_s** is because it's a safe version of the classic C library **strcpy** function. You should always use **strcpy_s** not **strcpy**.

By safe, I mean it includes the size of the target buffer, so it can't copy outside the buffer. Buffer overflow was a common programming problem for novice programmers with **strcpy** and other string functions.

The **sltoa()** function converts the int value to a string and returns a pointer to it. This string was created in the buffer convbuff. Both it and **sltoa** are in the lib.c file. The net result of the **strcpy_s** call is that the message field in the particular TextSprite holds the string characters of the score.

DrawTextSprites is very short.

```
void DrawTextSprites() {
   for (int i = 0; i < MAXTEXTSPRITES;i++) {
      struct TextSprite * psprite = &sprites[i];
      if (psprite->active--) {
         TextAt(psprite->x, psprite->y--, psprite->message);
         if (!psprite->y) {
            psprite->active = 0;
         }
      }
   }
}
```

It loops through the sprites and if a text sprite is active, decrements active and calls TextAt to draw the value on the screen, decrementing the y coordinate so the score moves up slowly.

If the sprite hits the top of the screen, active is set to 0 and that stops it being drawn any more.

A really stupid bug

Can you spot the bug in the above code? Something was overwriting all my text sprites and new ones weren't being added and displayed. C makes it easy to do this and I managed to add a bug by trying to be too clever.

It was this line.

```
if (psprite->active--) {
```

So if a sprite is active (i.e. active is >0) then it does the TextAt and decrements active at the same time. But when active was 0, it would correctly skip the TextAt but still decremented active which now had a value of -1 and so would keep on decrementing active . D'oh!

-1 in decimal (32 bit signed numbers) in hexadecimal is 0xFFFFFFFF.

This is the fixed version of that if statement.

```
if (psprite->active) {
   TextAt(psprite->x, psprite->y--, psprite->message);
   psprite->active--;
   if (!psprite->y) {
      psprite->active = 0;
   }
}
```

It was easy to find the problem. I put a breakpoint on the MoveAsteroids() call in GameLoop(). When the program reached here it stopped and I had it display memory.

When you are debugging it's on the Top menu (Debug) then Windows then memory on the pop-up menu. In the address bar I typed sprites and could see the bytes.

I then kept pressing F10 to run each function then stop. first MoveAsteroids then RotatePlayerShip etc. After each one I could see if the sprites memory had been overwritten.

After DrawEverything() I could see lots of FF values in sprites so I put a breakpoint here against DrawEverything() and pressed F5 until it got there then I pressed F11 to step into it.

I then did F10 to take me through DrawAsteroids, DrawPlayerShip until DrawTextSprites and I saw the values change. I put a breakpoint on DrawTextSprites and did F5 to get here again. F5 runs it until it hits a breakpoint. Pressing F11 then stepped into it and I could see what had happened.

As a general rule of thumb, when something starts going wrong look at your most recent code changes first.

The main program is now over 1,300 lines long so viewing it to spot bugs isn't easy and gets harder as the program gets bigger.

Another debugging technique, is comment out functions one at a time and run the program. If the bug doesn't occur then it's a good guess that it happened in the last commented out function and you can focus your attention on it.

A bug fixing Strategy

Bugs are a way of life in programming, so you have to be able to fix them. Here's a two line strategy to help you do that.

1. Find out how to replicate the bug. You can't fix it if you can't make it happen.
2. Use the various techniques I've mentioned to zoom in and find out which function it happens in and then step through the function to find the line where it occurs.

I have two 21" monitors on my PC. That way I can run the program on one screen and step through it in the Visual Studio debugger on the other screen. If you have a large screen that can fit both your program and Visual Studio in without them overlapping then that's just as good.

Files for this chapter.

The zip file containing everything is asteroids_ch45.zip.

Chapter 46. Adding Level Structure

So far we just hit the 'a' key to add asteroids then shoot them until we lose all our lives. We want to make it into more of a game by adding levels to increase the difficulty.

We're going to do this fairly simply. We have several possible ways of doing this.

1. Increase the number of asteroids.
2. Increase the size of asteroids.
3. Mix 1 and 2.
4. Add alien ships.
5. Increase the speed of asteroids.

I decided to have a maximum of 50 levels. If you get through all 50 then you have beaten the game. At this point it's a bit hard to figure out what makes the game harder. Is moving asteroids faster or adding bigger asteroids what makes it more difficult?

This is what the struct Level looks like.

```
struct level {
    int nums[4]; // how many of each size of asteroid
    int aliens; // how many aliens
    float factor; // from 1.0 to 1.5 - multiply asteroid speed by this
};
```

So we need 5 **ints** and a **float** to define a level. I used Excel to create the levels. That way I could assign a weight to each of the six factors and calculate a total 'difficulty' weight for each level and try and get balance in the progression.

When you are designing a game, adding balance is a hard thing to do. Too easy and people will finish it quickly; too hard and they'll give up. You have to get something in between or give something back like - "every five alien ships killed gets you an extra life". Power-ups can be a good balancing factor.

Off the top of my head I can think of several ways of doing power-ups.

1. After a certain score you gain an extra ship's cannon, with both at an angle rather than shooting straight ahead.
2. A random thing moves across the screen. If you shoot it, you gain a smart bomb that destroys everything on screen at once when triggered.
3. Or you move into a floating shield generator and it gives you a shield that lets you absorb hits without losing a life but it depletes with each hit until it's gone.
4. You get an enhanced hyper-jump that can be used every 1.5 seconds instead of three seconds.

Power-ups can be triggered after certain levels, scores achieved or total asteroids destroyed. As well as positive power-ups there can be other hazards such as a black hole. It starts sucking everything towards it and swallows them: aliens, asteroids and your ship. You jump away and use thrust to try and keep you away until it evaporates.

Yes this has evolved from asteroids though the fundamental game mechanisms are still there. It'll be 40 years since Asteroids first appeared and adding on all these features makes it a new game. Breakout appeared in the mid-1970s but the idea was completely revamped by Arkanoid that appeared ten years after that.

Now from my experiences four big asteroids on screen at once is starting to get very tough. So we build up to asteroids at 1.5 speed with 4 large asteroids and three alien ships.

Making Life Easier for yourself

I love using Excel to prepare data structures. You can create complex structures with C syntax so you just copy and paste them directly into your program's source code.

Let me show an example using levels. I've used the struct level as a model and populated an Excel spreadsheet with 50 levels of data. Now I want to get that into my C program.

In C99 you initialise a struct variable such as level like this:

```
struct level onelevel = { .factor = (float)1.0, .aliens = 0, .nums = { 3,3,0,0 } };
```

You can put that in an array so here are three of them. They have the same values but you get the idea.

```
struct level mylevels3[3] = {
{.factor = (float)1.0,.aliens = 0,.nums = { 3,3,0,0 } },
{.factor = (float)1.0,.aliens = 0,.nums = { 3,3,0,0 } },
{.factor = (float)1.0,.aliens = 0,.nums = { 3,3,0,0 } } };
```

So having populated my spreadsheet with values. I can now have it create the whole strings. *Note if you don't know Excel formulas, you concatenate strings with & not +.*

I had the six fields (4 asteroids, number aliens, speed factor) in columns b-g, starting at row 5. This was the formula I pasted into cell M5.

```
="{.factor =(float)"&G5&", .aliens="&F5&", .nums = {"&B5&","&C5&","&D5&","&E5&"}}, // Level "&A5
```

I then copied and pasted that in successive rows all the way from m5 down to m54 and pasted that entire string into levels.c. I added a { at the start and a matching } at the end and removed the last comma. It took ten minutes to create a struct with all my data in this way. It's much easier and way less error-prone than doing it manually!

The idea is to put the levels data in its own file levels.c,, create a header file levels.h and then declare the levels array as **extern**. It means levels.c only gets compiled once.

So in the main program we add these definitions.

```
#include "levels.h"
#define MAXLEVELS 50
extern struct level levels[MAXLEVELS];
```

In levels.h we have these declarations.

```c
struct level {
    int nums[4]; // how many of each size of asteroid
    int aliens; // how many aliens
    float factor; // from 1.0 to 1.5 - multiply astereoid speed by this
};
```

In levels.c we have this less 45 rows I snipped.

```c
#include "levels.h"
struct level levels[50] = {
{.factor = (float)1,.aliens = 0,.nums = { 3,3,0,0 } }, // Level 1
{.factor = (float)1,.aliens = 0,.nums = { 3,3,1,0 } }, // Level 2
{.factor = (float)1,.aliens = 0,.nums = { 3,3,1,0 } }, // Level 3
   ...
{.factor = (float)1.5,.aliens = 3,.nums = { 5,5,3,4 } }, // Level 49
{.factor = (float)1.5,.aliens = 3,.nums = { 5,5,4,4 } } // Level 50
```

It can be a toss up whether you want to hard code config data like this in the program as I've done. You might instead write a program to convert it to a binary file and read it in via a resource manager. A resource manager lets you compress or encrypt data which makes it harder for game hackers to decompile and access your resources.

You wouldn't include the C struct code in if you used a resource manager. Instead you'd create a C program to read the C source data e.g. 1,0,3,3,0,0 (the first line's values) and write that out to a binary file.

Adding Lives

We've already got player.lives which is set to 3 and show three ships in the bottom left of the screen. But we now need to build in the code for supporting this.

Little things like when a level ends, it's either because the player ship got blown up or all on screen objects were destroyed. For now this means asteroids but in the future it will mean alien ships as well.

This is how main now looks.

```
int main(int argc, char * args[])
{
    InitLogging("biglog.txt");
    InitSetup();
    if (errorCount) {
        return -1;
    }
    do {
        InitGame();
        while (Player.lives){
            GameLoop();
            if (CloseFlag) break;
        };
        if(!Player.lives) break;
    } while (!CloseFlag);
    CloseLogging();
    FinishOff();
    return 0;
}
```

CloseFlag is an int that is set to 0 in InitSetup(). If you hit the escape kety, it's set to 1 and the game finishes immediately.

Within GameLoop() before the while (ProcessEvents()) there's this code:

```
InitLevel(gameLevel);
frameCount = 0;
while (frameCount < 59) {
    RenderTexture(textures[PLBACKDROP], 0, 0);
    DrawTextSprites();
    RenderEverything();
```

}

This draws a 2 line banner in large text that scrolls up for one second before the level begins.

The InitLevel function gets the number of asteroids etc. from the levels array for this game level.

```
void InitLevel(int glevel) {
   ReInitGame(); // Clear BEATT Bullets Explosions Asteroids Thrust and Text
   struct level * thislevel = &levels[glevel];
   for (int sizeindex = 0; sizeindex <4; sizeindex++) {
      int numtoadd=thislevel->nums[sizeindex];
      if (numtoadd) {
         for (int aindex = 0; aindex < numtoadd; aindex++) {
            AddAsteroid(sizeindex);
         }
      }
   }
   speedfactor = thislevel->factor;
   DrawLevelStart();
}
```

DrawLevelStart makes use of two Textsprites to display the large upwards scrolling banner. To do this I modified the print routines to accept a textFactor; an int that multiplies the target rectangle in printch. These take an extra parameter.

Note that the last line of printch uses textFactor to work out the larger widths. If textFactor is 2 then the character widths will be 2 * 13 = 26.

```
// print single char c at rect target
void printch(char c, SDL_Rect * target, int textFactor) {
   int start = (c - '!');
```

```
    if (c != ' ') {
        sourceRect.h = 23;
        sourceRect.w = 12;
        sourceRect.x = start * 12;
        sourceRect.y = 0;
        SDL_RenderCopy(renderer, textures[TEXTTEXTURE],
&sourceRect, target);
    }
    (*target).x += (13*textFactor); // in this bitmap font, chars are 13 pixels width
}
// print string text at x,y pixel coords
void TextAt(int atX, int atY, char * msg,int textFactor) {
    destRect.h = 23*textFactor;
    destRect.w = 12*textFactor;
    destRect.x = atX;
    destRect.y = atY;
    for (int i = 0; i < (int)strlen(msg); i++) {
        printch(msg[i], &destRect,textFactor);
    }
}
```

The DrawTextSprites now includes the textFactor in the TextSprite struct and means you can have multiple text sizes (same font and colour though!) on screen at the same time.

That takes care of the game level structure. In the next chapter we'll finally add the alien ships.

Aliens?

Though the levels struct includes aliens, I've not added them in this chapter. For that you'll have to wait to the next chapter.

Changes to Text Sprites

As well as the larger size, I split the AddTextSprite into three functions. The one that does most of the work is AddTextSpriteAt and this takes a string and creates a sprite that displays it at the specified x,y.

I've added AddTextSpriteInt and AddTextSpriteString. Neither of these passes in the x coordinate, instead calculating it centred horizontally from the string length. AddTextSpriteInt calls AddTextString which calls AddTextSpriteAt.

There's a call to the AddTextSpriteAt to show the 50 point score near where the target was destroyed.

```
// This creates a Text sprite at the x,y coordinates
void AddTextSpriteAt(char * value, int x, int y, int textfactor) {
   int spriteindex = findFreeSprite();
   if (spriteindex == -1 || y<20) return;
   struct TextSprite * psprite = &sprites[spriteindex];
   psprite->x = x;
   psprite->y = y;
   psprite->active = 60;
   psprite->textFactor = textfactor;
   strcpy_s(psprite->message, sizeof(psprite->message), value);
   numsprites++;
}
// This centres the text horizontally
void AddTextSpriteString(char * value, int y, int textfactor) {
   int textlen = strlen(value) * 13*textfactor;
   int x = (WIDTH - textlen) / 2; // x location for string to be centred
   AddTextSpriteAt(value, x, y, textfactor);
}
// This uses an int
void AddTextSpriteInt(int value, int y, int textfactor) {
   AddTextSpriteString(sltoa(value), y, textfactor);
}
```

It's not unusual to evolve code like this as you develop it. I could have just copied the body from the AddTextSpriteAt into the other two functions but having the same eight lines three times is wasteful. It violates a programming principle called Once and Once Only.

Game play problem

I found that quite often asteroids were appearing so near the player ship that it got hit and blew up before the player had a chance to react. This despite the asteroid not being placed in a non-empty space.

So I implemented a restricted area that is 150 x 150 pixels square in the centre. To save calculation time I defined it using #defines. If you decide to change the size of this area just change ZONESIZE and the other four values will be correct.

```
#define ZONESIZE 150
#define ZONELEFT (SCREENWIDTH-ZONESIZE)/2
#define ZONERIGHT ZONELEFT+ZONESIZE
#define ZONETOP (SCREENHEIGHT-ZONESIZE)/2
#define ZONEBOTTOM ZONETOP+ZONESIZE
```

I then added a function InCentre which returns 1 if the x,y coordinates are within this restricted area. So AddAsteroids now checks not only that it's putting an Asteroid in an empty space but also not in the central restricted area.

It still won't stop a fast moving asteroid hitting you but most of the time, you'll be safe.

Another change was renaming the CoolDown function to DoCoolDown. Having a variable with the same name as a function is just madness! Well even though the different cases allowed it, it's easy to get the two mixed up.

Finally as I've used 13 in several places as the width of one character in our bitmap font, I've made it into a #DEFINE CHARWIDTH 13.

Yet another Bug!

While checking the source code for each chapter, I compiled it and ran the program to make sure it's ok. The one in this chapter with asteroids13.c worked great except no bullets were being fired. I looked through the code but nothing sprang out.

I compared the asteroids13.c file against the final version named asteroids.c. There were 1500 lines in asteroids13.c and 2168 in Asteroids.c. I'd added extra code for the alien ships in the next chapter and extra comments as well.

When you have a situation like this, a code comparison utility is very very handy. In my case I used WinMerge. There are many out there, both open source and commercial. WinMerge is open source and a must have utility for occasions like this.

You just give it the two files and it highlights all the differences. This was the line that broke my code.

It was in the first line of the function DoFireBullet which gets called when you press the Fire key. In case you can't make it out, the one on the left (asteroids13.c) is this

void DoFireBullet() {
   if (playerBulletCount = MAXPLAYERBULLETS) return;
   int index = -1;
   for (int i = 0; i<MAXBULLETS; i++) {

and the one on the right (asteroids.c) is this.

void DoFireBullet() {

```
    if (playerBulletCount == MAXPLAYERBULLETS) return;
    int index = -1;
    for (int i = 0; i<MAXBULLETS; i++) {
```

It's that bug I warned you about, A comparison == becoming an assignment =. D'oh!

I've no idea how the == became = but as this assigned MAXPLAYERBULLETS (the value 16) to playerBulletCount, it would always return hence no bullets were fired until it was fixed.

Files for this chapter.

The zip file containing everything is asteroids_ch46.zip. Note this also contains difficultylevels.xlsx the Excel file with the levels.

Chapter 47. Alien Ships!

There's a 64 x 64 pixels called alien.png. I modified the genmask.c program to generate a mask alien.msk. Remember the Github project for this includes all masks, graphics and sounds and source code. You've bought the book and can use those Github assets as you wish. If you make a million bucks, send me a tenner (£10) as a thank you!

Adding this need you to increase NUMTEXTURES, texturenames etc. The image is in the images folder, I added "images/alien.png" to texturenames.

```
#define MAXALIENS 3
byte alienmask[64][64];
struct alien {
    SDL_Rect r;
    int type; // 3
    int active;
    int movedir;
    float x, y;
    float xvel, yvel;
    int xtime, ytime;
    int ttl;
};
struct alien aliens[MAXALIENS];
```

There's nothing here that you haven't seen before. Most of the code for MoveAlien comes from MoveAsteroid but without rotations. Likewise DrawAlien is similar, apart from the size which is set to ALIENSHIPWIDTH/ALIENSHIPHEIGHT. These two #defines are the same but if you ever wanted to use graphics that weren't square, all you'd need is to change the #defines.

Alien Artificial intelligence

Asteroids are given a direction in which to move at a velocity and it never changes. Alien ships have two purposes in life; avoid asteroids and shoot at you though they seem better at the latter than the former.

Programming the second one is by far the easier. However rather than try to program evasive manoeuvres into the alien ships, if they register a threat then they shoot at it.

Alien ships are inferior to our human ship and can only have 8 bullets in play at once (per ship) as defined by #define MAXBULLETSPERALIEN 8.

Because of this limit, we must track how many bullets each ship has fired. If it has 8 in play then tough. No more.

The struct bullet has a field playerbullet which does our dirtywork for us.

It has 4 values- -1 means its a player bullet and 0-MAXALIENS-1 means it's an alien bullet. I defined the enum BulletOwner and the first of the four values bplayer has an initial value of -1.

Note also that our bullets struct has to accommodate all bullets so I've defined a new MAXTOTALBULLETS MAXBULLETS + (MAXBULLETSPERALIEN * MAXALIENS). That's 16 + (8 * 3) = 40. Where I used MAXBULLETS I've changed it to MAXTOTALBULLETS.

One thing I found was that the player could fire more bullets, so I added the CountBullets() function that is called each frame. It keeps two totals, alien bullets and player bullets.

When is a function not a function?

For the bullet firing we need to determine the direction. For that we need a sgn function, sometimes called signum. If you pass in a positive number it returns 1, for 0 it returns 0 and for a negative number it returns -1. Now we could define it as a function like this:

```
int sgn(int x) {
    if (x <0) return -1;
    if (!x) return 0;
    return 1;
}
```

But if we wanted a float or double version we'd have to do one for each of the different types.

However there is another way. We define a macro using #define.

```
#define sgn(x) (x < 0) ? -1 : (x > 0)
```

Remember macros just substitute anywhere it sees sgn(x) with (x < 0) ? -1 : (x > 0).

So if you have

```
int a = sgn(y);
```

It will actually compile it as.

```
int a = (y < 0) ? -1 : (y > 0);
```

Plus it works with int, float, double etc. The only downsize is that if you call sgn() in 20 places, you get the (x < 0) ? -1 : (x > 0) code 20 times. In that case functions may be better as it would produce less code!

Flashing Alien

I added two int variables:

flashFlag
flashTimer

Remember, all the timer variables are actually counters.

Given that the game is running at 60 FPS, having something flash say three times per second, this bit of code at the start of the GameLoop's while (ProcessEvents()) has a flashFlag variable.

```
flashTimer++;
if (flashTimer == 20)
{
    flashFlag = 1 - flashFlag;
    flashTimer = 0;
}
```

The flashTimer counts up once per frame up to 20, in 1/3rd of a second. At that point the flashFlag goes from 0 to 1 or 1 to 0 and the FlashTimer is reset to 0.

So during each second the flashFlag is 1 for 1/3rd of a second then 0 for the next third and then 1 again and this repeats all through the game.

So if you want something to "flash" just print it when flashFlag is 1. In the DrawAlienShips code, you'll see this.

```
if (flashFlag) {
    SDL_RenderCopy(renderer, textures[TEXTUREALIENSHIP], &spriterect, &target);
}
```

As we're clearing the screen 60 times a second then drawing everything, if flashFlag is 0 means it doesn't get drawn.

That's all it takes to have the alien ships flash. Of course they all flash at the same time which doesn't look that great. So let's make them flash individually. To do this I added a flShow and a flTimer to each alien struct.

The flTimer i set to a random number between 0 and 14 (defined by ALIENFLASHFRAMES which is 15. Everytimne round the GameLoop a function called UpdateTimers() is called.

I've put flashTimer in there, but the more important bit is the updating of the aliens flTimer. For a value of 15 this means each alien ship is visible for15 frames (1/4 second) then invisible for 15. So it's flashing twice a second. Because of the initial flTimer seed, the aliens are not flashing in sync.

I've moved the alien flash code into an updateTimers() function. It still toggles the flashFlag three times a second but also toggles each alien's flShow at the specified rate.

```
void UpdateTimers() {
   flashTimer++;
   if (flashTimer == 20)
   {
      flashFlag = 1 - flashFlag;
      flashTimer = 0;
   }
   if (numaliens > 0) {
      for (int i = 0; i < MAXALIENS; i++) {
         struct alien * palien = &aliens[i];
         if (palien->active) {
            palien->flTimer++;
            if (palien->flTimer == ALIENFLASHFRAMES) {
               palien->flTimer = 0;
               palien->flShow = 1 - palien->flShow;
```

```
        }
      }
     }
    }
   }
  }
}
```

Adding a Shield control

I found the game getting a bit hard so added a game balance feature.

The player's ship now has a shield that saves your ship. Holding S down activates the shield. While it's active, nothing can blow up the player ship.

The shield drains power when in use and when the power runs out, the shield drops. It then has to recharge.

We'll have a shieldFlag that is 1 when the shield is active. But the shield only has 100 units of power.

Every frame the shield is active drains the shieldStrength by 1. When it reaches 0 the shield collapses.

When the shield is inactive it charges up the shieldStrength by 1 every three frames.

Drawing the Shield

I chose to modify the DrawPlayerShip() function by calling a DrawShield function from within it. It draws circles around the player ship by calling a DrawCircle function that I found on Stack Overflow.

I've added a link to the StackOverflow question in my source as a comment. It's a courtesy and I recommend you do it for any code you get from there.

Since February 2016, all code published on Stackoverflow is covered by the MIT License. You can read about the Stackoverflow website licence change here.

The long and the short of it is you are free to use code from Stackoverflow as I have done.

Note that it only draws the shield circles when the ShieldStrength is above 10. The + 32 on the x and y are because all coordinates of objects are for the top left hand corner. The circles have to be drawn centred on the middle of the player's ship.

```
// Draws throbbing circle round ship
void DisplayShield(SDL_Rect * target) {
   if (shieldFlag && shieldStrength >10) {
      SDL_SetRenderDrawColor(renderer, 0xff, 0xff, 0xff, 0xff);
      DrawCircle(renderer, target->x + (SHIPWIDTH/2), target->y + (SHIPHEIGHT/2), shieldRadius);
      shieldRadius += 2;
      if (shieldRadius == 46) {
         shieldRadius = 38;
```

```
        }
    }
    if (shieldStrength < 100) {
        TextAt(target->x + 10, target->y + 58, sltoa(shieldStrength), 0.67);
    }
}
```

This also prints the shieldStrength underneath the ship when it's less than 100.

I changed the TextAt function so the TextFactor parameter (the last one) can take floats. This lets me scale the text down as well as up and here the shield strength is printed in two thirds of normal size text.

Generally pixel graphic drawing routines can be relatively slow so at some point I'll time this. If it turns out to be too slow, it might be easier to draw the five circles (of radius, 38, 40, 42, 44 and 46) as graphics and then draw them using SDL_RenderCopy.

There's no code in this chapter, it's all at the end of chapter 48 and that is the final version.

Chapter 48. The High Score

This will be the last feature I'm going to add to the game. After that it's tidying up, bit of timing and polishing and that's it.

The high score table will be displayed before each game and after it. It's going to have ten entries each holding initials, a score, the highest level cleared and the date. We need a struct to hold each entry and an array of ten of those structs.

```
#define NUMSCORES 10
struct HighScoreEntry {
    char initials[4];
    int score;
    int d, m, y;
  int level;
};
struct HighScoreEntry highscores[NUMSCORES];
void InitHighScores() {
    memset(highscores, 0, sizeof(highscores));
}
```

The InitHighScores is called from InitSetup, not InitGame as we want the scores to survive between games. To do that the highscores are written to a text file in the function WriteHighScores and read in (in ReadHighScores) when the program starts.

To keep it simple, I saved each HighScoreEntry as a 19 character string in this format.

DDMMYYYYIIILLSSSSSS

Where DD is day (01-31), MM = month (01-31), YYYY = year (2018) II are the initials e.g. DHB, LL is the level (00-50) and SSSSSS is the score with leading zeroes e.g. 000500.

C is not the best language for manipulating strings.

This is what it takes to read in the 19 character strings from the highscores.txt file. The StrConv converts a string that's part of a longer string to an integer; you specify the start and length. StrCopyTo copies one string to another and adds a terminating zero.

These two functions are explicitly copying a number of chars. The copied strings have no terminating zero as C strings normally do so that's why I wrote them.

Note that StrCopyTo writes to a char * but the Initials type is a char[4] hence the need for the cast to char * when StrCopyTo is called.

```c
int StrConv(char * line, int start, int len) {
    char buffer[20];
    if (len > sizeof(buffer))
        len = sizeof(buffer) - 1; // error check length
    for (int i = 0; i < len; i++) {
        buffer[i] = line[start++];
    }
    buffer[start] = 0;
    return atoi(buffer);
}
void StrCopyTo(char * dest, char * line, int start, int len) {
    for (int i = 0; i < len; i++) {
        dest[i] = line[start++];
    }
    dest[start] = 0;
    return;
}
int ReadHighScores() {
    InitHighScores();
    FILE * fscores;
    char line[20]; // long enough for 17 char string plus trailing 0
    int error = fopen_s(&fscores, highscoreFN, "rt");
    if (error != 0) return 0;
    numHighScores = 0;
    while (fgets(line, sizeof(line), fscores)) {
        if (strlen(line) == 18) {
            highscores[numHighScores].d = StrConv(line, 0, 2);
            highscores[numHighScores].m = StrConv(line, 2, 2);
            highscores[numHighScores].y = StrConv(line, 4, 4);
            StrCopyTo((char *)&highscores[numHighScores].initials, line, 8, 3);
```

```
            highscores[numHighScores++].score = StrConv(line, 11, 6);
            if (numHighScores == 10) break;
        }
        else break;
    }

    fclose(fscores);
    return numHighScores;
}
```

So the game can now persist and reuse high scores. We need to capture a high score during play and display them.

Displaying the high scores

It uses the same mini-loop technique to display the high scores as scrolling text does.

In the main loop, DisplayHighScores() runs until the player presses a key. Well not the escape key as that exits the program, but any other key will exit the loop and then start the game.

The high score is ten rows with the Date Initials, Level and Score and each line flashes one by one.

```
void DisplayHighScores() {
    char buffer[50];
    int flashIndex;
    int hsTimer;
      flashIndex = 1;
    hsTimer = 0;
    while (ProcessEvents()) {
        UpdateTimers(); // needed or flashFlag doesn't work
        int y = 130;
        if (CloseFlag || fireFlag) return;
        RenderTexture(textures[PLBACKDROP], 0, 0);
        TextAt(350, 30, "High Scores", 3.0f);
```

```
        if (flashFlag) {
           TextAt(400, 650, "Press space to start", 1.0f);
        }
        for (int i = 0; i < 10; i++) {
            struct HighScoreEntry * entry = &highscores[i];
            if (entry->score) {
                sprintf_s(buffer, sizeof(buffer) - 1, "%02d/%02d/%4d %3s %06d", entry->d, entry->m, entry->y, entry->initials, entry->score);
            }
            else {
                sprintf_s(buffer, sizeof(buffer) - 1, "--/--/---------000000");
            }
            if (flashIndex != i) {
                TextAt(250, y, buffer, 1.0f);
            }
            y += 50;
        }
        RenderEverything();
        hsTimer++;
        if (hsTimer==18) {
            flashIndex++;
            hsTimer = 0;
            if (flashIndex == 10) flashIndex = 0;
        }
   }
}
```

There's nothing much new here. It uses the ProcessEvents like in the GameLoop; think of the high scores as a different type of game loop. It also uses the flashTimer, and to make that work it has to call UpdateTimers() each frame.

It exits if the space or escape keys are pressed which set the fireFlag (space bar) or CloseFlag variables.

The hsTimer is incremented every frame and when it reaches 18 resets to 0 and the local flashIndex variable is incremented. It's used to blank each of the high score entries, one by one to get the flashing effect. The 18/60 frequency is different to the flashFlag (20/60 frequency) used here to flash the "Press space to start" message at the foot of the high scores.

In the sprintf_s, the various format strings control the output. %02d displays an int with a leading 0 like 08, and %06d does the same for the scores like 003500.

Entering the High Score

Finally when the game has finished, if your high score beats any of the scores in the high score table, you are invited to enter your initials. This again is done in a screen like the GameLoop based on a while(ProcessEvents()) loop.

It's one of the longer functions because of the mini loop inside which just looks for key presses. Also it uses a separate function SetTodaysDate to get today's date in an entry.

The while(SDL_PollEvent loop looks for three keys, with scoreIndex 0,1 and 2. It uses this to index into the newInitials array. This has four elements with the last one set to 0, so newInitials can also be accessed as a c tert string and displayed on screen in the third TextAt.

The coolDown is used to show the third initial for one second, otherwise it would exit before displaying it.

The scoreIndex is the index (0-9)

```
void SetTodaysDate(struct HighScoreEntry * entry) {
    time_t t = time(NULL);
    struct tm rawtime;
    time(&t);
    if (localtime_s(&rawtime, &t) == 0) {
```

```
        entry->d = rawtime.tm_mday;
        entry->m = rawtime.tm_mon + 1;
        entry->y = rawtime.tm_year + 1900;
    }
}
// Gets initials and puts in high score if score high enough
void CheckHighScore() {
    int scoreIndex = -1;
    int Entered = 0;
    for (int i = NUMSCORES-1; i >=0; i--) { //check reverse order
        if (score > highscores[i].score) {
            scoreIndex = i;
        }
    }
    if (scoreIndex == -1) return;
    // Score goo enough to be in high score table
    char newInitials[4] = {'-','-','-',0 };
    coolDown = 0;
    int scoreIndex=-1;
    while (!Entered) {
        RenderTexture(textures[PLBACKDROP], 0, 0);
        UpdateTimers();
        TextAt(350, 30, "New High Score!", 3.0f);
        TextAt(200, 200, "Enter Initials:",1.5F);
        TextAt(500, 200, newInitials,1.5F);
        if (flashFlag) {
            TextAt(350, 5000, "Press three keys", 1.0f);
        }
        RenderEverything();
        while (SDL_PollEvent(&event)) {
```

```
            if (coolDown == 0) {
               switch (event.type) {
               case SDL_KEYDOWN:
                  keypressed = event.key.keysym.sym;
                  if (keypressed >= SDLK_a && keypressed <= SDLK_z) {
                     scoreIndex++;
                     newInitials[scoreIndex] = keypressed - 32; // A--Z
                     if (scoreIndex == 2) {
                        coolDown = 50; // Time for 3rd letter to be seen on screen
                     } // if ScoreIndex
                  } // if keypressed
               } // switch
            } // if
         }
         if (coolDown > 0) {
            coolDown--;
            if (coolDown == 0) {
               Entered = 1;
               break;
            }
         }
      }
   }
   // Shuffle all highscores after new one, down one
   for (int i = NUMSCORES-1; i > scoreIndex; i--) {
      highscores[i] = highscores[i - 1];
   }
   // Set new scores
   struct HighScoreEntry * entry = &highscores[scoreIndex];
   SetTodaysDate(entry);
   for (int i = 0; i < 4; i++) {
```

```
        entry->initials[i] = newInitials[i];
    }
    entry->score = score;
}
```

Files for this chapter.

The zip file containing everything is asteroids_ch48.zip. This is the final working version of the game and almost 2,200 lines long in **asteroids.c**.

Remember you are free to use this code as you wish for creating your own games.

Chapter 49. Finishing off

If you've got this far then congratulations. You're probably a better programmer than me if you've gone over every line of code!

Some timings:

Timings vary according to the hardware on your desktop/laptop etc. I believe that all but the oldest PCs should be able to run this at 60 frames per second.

I created another #define TIMEGAMELOOP.

When it's defined the captions shows the average time per frame. It's timed over a whole 60 frames and the time is divided by a million to get microseconds.

```
#ifdef TIMEGAMELOOP
    counter++;
    numTimeSlices++;
    stopTimer(&s);
    totalTime += getElapsedTime(&s);
    if (counter == 60) {
        sprintf_s(timebuff, sizeof(timebuff) - 1, "%12.8f ", totalTime/numTimeSlices/1000000);
        counter = 0;
    }
    startTimer(&s);
#endif
```

On my PC it seems to take about 60 microseconds per frame. Given that we have almost 17,000 microseconds available for each frame that means there's no possibility of this overruning a frame.

The only way overrunning has been possible if the collision detection doesn't trigger the destruction of objects and large asteroids pass over other large asteroids; that reduced the frame rate to 4 frames per seond so those took 250 milliseconds.

Chapter 50. Obtaining Source code and Resources

All the game files, zipped up into three zip files (graphics.zip, sounds.zip and examples.zip) can be download from Github.

The four files are:

1. Graphics.zip – All game graphics
2. Sounds.zip – All game sounds
3. Examples.zip – All C example source code

There are also 14 asteroids files with names like asteroids_ch27.zip etc. These correspond to the state of the asteroids source code at the end of the specified chapter. Each of these contains the exe, sources, images, sounds and sdl dlls. The last of these files is asteroids_ch48.zip. This has the final version.

You are enturely free to change the graphics and use your owna nd the same is true for the sound files.

If you enhance the game substantially, let me know and send a copy of your source code and I'll add it to the site with a link back to you!

Running asteroids outside of Visual Studio

When running a program from Visual Studio in debug mode, it starts as if the program is run from the project folder; i.e. the one with all your sources. That's why images and sounds folders are below this, at the same level as the debug folder.

When running from a folder, say c:\asteroids or d:\asteroids, you need the exes, masks and dlls all in that folder. And sounds and images folders located below the asteroids. E.G. c:\asteroids\images and c:\asteroids\sounds

These files and folders should be in the asteroids folder:

alien.msk

am1.msk
am2.msk
am3.msk
am4.msk
asteroids.exe
bullet.msk
images
libpng16-16.dll
playership.msk
SDL2.dll
SDL2_image.dll
SDL2_mixer.dll
sounds
zlib1.dll

Printed in Great Britain
by Amazon